Get Out of the Way and Let Kids Learn!

How We Can Transform
Schools and Reintroduce
Natural Learning

By Carl Rust

Table of Contents

Foreword: What if we are the problem?   Pg. 5

Chapter 1 - My Learning Journey   Pg.15

Chapter 2 - Should children be grouped by age in grade levels?   Pg. 52

Chapter 3 - Should children learn the same thing at the same time?   Pg. 65

Chapter 4 - Is Play an extra? Is it less important than instruction?   Pg. 77

Chapter 5 - How much should children and their families be involved in decision-making?   Pg. 84

Chapter 6 - Are testing and grades necessary to determine what children have learned and guide instruction? Pg. 91

Chapter 7 - Does coercion and compliance lead to good citizenship and a happy life?   Pg. 102

Chapter 8 - Do we need school buildings and classrooms?   Pg. 110

Chapter 9 - Do we need to supervise children to keep them safe?   Pg. 117

Chapter 10 - Is the best way to learn is to sit and listen to a teacher talk?   Pg. 122

Chapter 11 - When and how will change happen? Pg. 131

Chapter 12 - The dazzling or dismal future.   Pg. 152

References   Pg. 156

Foreword: What if we are the problem?

I look around and see kids of different ages. Some are on computers, some drawing, some are talking to each other. The room is arranged somewhat like an office with 32 workstations in groups of 4 and 8. Several adults and children are playing a word game on ipads and phones. I walk into another large room and see several kids flopped on couches watching videos on ipads. At one table an adult is reading a book with a student. An adjoining small room holds some growing plants and 3 girls singing along with a YouTube video. A tiny room holds an electronic keyboard and a young boy is experimenting with the settings. Is this really school?

Imagine visiting your town you one hundred years ago. You walk around taking in the sights and sounds. You see some primitive automobiles, the beginnings of electricity, clothing that people wore, how they spoke to each other and you marvel at how different the world is today. You find yourself at the local hospital. How differently they do things! You find yourself feeling very glad that you live in a time when medical advances are a marvel and illnesses and injuries that might have killed you one hundred years ago are insignificant today.

Now you walk into the local school. Teachers are standing in front of the room talking and writing on chalkboards. Students are sitting at desks in rows passively taking notes or daydreaming. The clothes are different, the topics discussed may be different, but the methods and structure are very close to what we still have today in many classrooms. At specified times throughout the day a bell rings and students move to a different location to do a different activity. The people who make decisions about what goes on in the school are the teachers, administrators, and local school board. The students themselves, and even their parents, have very little say in what goes on.

How would we feel today if our doctor, dentist, and local hospital still used the same methods and structure of one hundred years ago, even though they knew better? There would be an uproar! People would protest! There would be demonstrations, petitions, and angry speeches.

Factory model schooling was designed to rank kids and figure out who was going to be a factory worker and who was going to be a manager, or maybe even a doctor, lawyer, teacher etc. The ones who were really good at the school game probably would be really good at any game, so could maneuver in the political waters that many professions require. A few slots were set aside for those especially talented in music, art, drama, writing or athletics and some misfits found refuge there. This system may have worked for most people at one time, while doing a lot of damage, but no longer are there tons of factory jobs and they are becoming scarcer as time moves on.

Educators have known for a long time that there are better ways to do school, but little has changed. Sure you can go into some classrooms in some schools and see more collaboration, more cooperative learning, more choices given to students as far as their activities and ways of completing work, but you can also find classrooms where other than the clothing or hairstyles you would be hard pressed to find a difference between now and 100 years ago.

I would also contend that even in the more open classrooms, the freedom is an illusion. The basic structure of the school is such that true freedom and authentic education is almost impossible. In an authoritarian structure, ultimately control is in the hands of a few adults and the little scraps of freedom that are given to students and their families are very limited.

I have been wondering lately if a lot of the problems we face in our world begin with schools. Could it be that poverty, crime, lack of participation in elections, discrimination of all kinds stem from the factory system of education that was purposely created to generate a docile, uninformed, unthinking working class?

Where else, but school, do you find people who have little freedom, can't leave, are told when to go to the restroom, when to eat, when to play, when to do everything? Where else, but school, do you find a place that you have to ask permission to sharpen a pencil, get a tissue, talk to the person next to you? The only other place I can think of that meets all those criteria is jail. You have maximum security jails and you have nice jails, but they are still jails and that is what schools have become. Some schools, some classrooms, some lunchrooms are nicer and more free than others, but in almost all of them the people who make the decisions are the adult staff with little or no input from the younger "students", even though the impact of the decisions being made is felt the most by the people who have little say. Almost all schools today operate on a traditional system. Some have changed little over the past 100 years and are clearly traditional. Others I call "enhanced traditional". These are basically adult controlled schools that use cooperation, collaboration, and technology to enhance the basic traditional instruction. Even private and charter schools follow the same basic operational philosophy. More and more free, holistic, and democratic schools and centers are popping up all over the world, but they are still in the minority.

Human beings are born curious. We learn constantly from the minute we take our first breath. We are constantly exploring the world and forming and testing hypotheses, gathering information and finding out who we are and how we fit into the world. Some people can sustain this curiosity and love of learning despite the structure of the school they find themselves in and some cannot.

For 13 years or more "students" are told what to do and when to do it. Freedom to choose is artificial and limited. You may get to choose whether to paint a horse or a cow, but you have to paint some kind of animal even if you hate to paint or don't like animals. In the freest classes you can make a diorama, or a video, or a play or whatever, but it has to be about the Middle Ages or Ancient Greece, even if you have no interest in any of that.

What if our current system of schooling is not really designed to produce creative, critical thinkers? What if it is doing exactly what it is designed to do? In *Weapons of Mass Instruction*, John Taylor Gatto systematically exposes the true intent of compulsory public education. Automatic compliance with authority without question, conforming to expected norms, comparing and ranking children, and identifying who will advance in society and who will not is the real agenda of public education, not developing each person's personal best.

For a great retelling of the history of compulsory education, see Ron Miller's book *What are Schools for?*

Year after year we see citizens who can't read well or solve math problems. Employers complain of a lack of skilled workers. People are apathetic and unwilling to contribute to society. They chase empty materialism, drugs, and sex. They crave entertainment. Is this due to school's failure to instruct students in correct ways? Maybe, but it could be that schools do exactly what they are supposed to do and dumb down our populace. If it is really because we are using faulty methods, why don't we change them? Could it be that the true purpose of compulsory public education is to reward and reinforce docility and compliance?

So the docile rule followers do fine. They may even like it. But the creative rebels are in torture. Sometimes the rebels withdraw and sullenly put forth as little effort as possible or they become violent, loud, abusive troublemakers. Kids that don't fit in either check out or act out. Rebellion cannot be allowed by the system so every attempt is made to bring the loud rebels into the fold. Punishment follows punishment until they either comply or are expelled or moved to another jail either nicer or stricter. Some creative types may be able to manipulate the system to their own advantage and find other ways to meet their learning needs and satisfy their innate curiosity. Some may come to crave being told what to do and when to do it. Some get kicked out or find their own path through homeschooling or some form of self-directed education. Some are saved by extra-curricular activities. In any case this is not the optimal way to learn and become a productive adult. In short, even though traditional school does not work for all students, there are few alternatives.

What if many of the practices and assumptions we implement at school actually stop learning in its tracks? Maybe if we get out of kids' way, their natural curiosity and desire to learn will kick in with amazing results.

There are 9 basic assumptions that are accepted as true by most educators, but need more scrutiny. I have stated these assumptions in a way that fits the reality I see in many schools. The teachers and administrators at a particular school may pay lip service to more progressive ideas, but if you watch what they do you will see that their actions support these assumptions.

1. Children should be grouped by age in grade levels.

2. All learners should learn the same thing at the same time.

3. Play is not as important as instruction and should be an extra.

4. Learners and their families should only be marginally involved in making decisions about how the school is run.

5. Testing and grades are necessary and help adults determine what students already know and what they need to learn.

6. Coercion and compliance leads to good citizenship and a peaceful life.

7. We need a school building with classrooms in order to maximize learning.

8. We need to supervise children in order to keep them safe.

9. The best way to learn something is to sit and listen to a teacher talk.

I will examine each of these assumptions plus more in this book, but first I want to give you a little background on me and my learning journey.

Chapter 1 - My Learning Journey

When I look back over my life I can see that I have been on a journey. A journey that shows no sign of ending. I am a learner. I learn new things every minute of every day. I also work with learners of various ages. It is my belief that you learn from the time you are born, at least up to your death, and depending on what happens in the afterlife, maybe after.

I have spent time playing different roles including student, wrangler on a dude ranch, bag boy, maintenance man, gas station attendant, YMCA worker, writer, actor, wrestler, artist, musician, husband, parent, grandparent, teacher and administrator. Sometimes these labels separate us from each other and we may come to think that the label defines us. "You are the teacher, so teach!" "I am the adult, you are the child, so do what I say!" These labels are facets of us, but they don't totally define us. We can rise above our labels and deal more effectively with our shared reality.

I have had the titles of director, teacher, and assistant principal, but I am no more important than the children or the other staff in the program. I have worked with amazing groups of people who all have their individual strengths and weaknesses as do the younger learners. I have been in the education business for 30 years and I know a few things that some others don't know, I have had experiences that they haven't had. But all the others know things I don't know and they have had experiences that I have never had. In the end, I am just another traveler down the road of life. We are all on a journey. A journey of learning. I guess the point I am driving at is that even though I have the title of director, I am just another person trying to make my way through life and by definition, learning.

Of course, learning begins at birth. That happened for me on January 11, 1957. My father, Howard, was a salesman, accountant, and all around witty guy. My mother Kathryn worked at home when I was little and then held various office jobs when I was older. She was the singer, the writer, the laugher. We always read, played games, sang and talked at our house. I didn't know then how lucky I was to have parents and older siblings (much older than me and out of the house by the time I was 3) and other family who read, played cards and board games, and talked and debated each other.

As far as I can remember we always had a television. I grew up with the idiot box. In Lima, Ohio, we only had a handful of choices; the three major networks and PBS I think. We had TV stations that broadcasted from Lima, Bowling Green, Columbus, Dayton, Toledo and Fort Wayne. We had an antenna outside and reception was very dependent on the weather. I liked westerns, Andy Griffith, Dick Van Dyke, Gilligan's Island, Get Smart, Ed Sullivan and later on Star Trek. Old movies on the weekends sometimes were interesting to me. On Saturday there were cartoons in the morning and Big Time Wrestling at noon, but there were vast periods of time when nothing was on that I liked. Which may have been just as well, because then I played outside or read. I liked mystery stories and comic books. I discovered Sherlock Holmes at some point. My parents also subscribed to a series of books about the Happy Hollisters who were a family that solved mysteries together. I had subscriptions to several Marvel comic books when I was young and liked to buy used ones when I had the chance.

I always played outside with the other kids in the neighborhood. We played after school and all day during the summer. We rode bikes, went to the local playgrounds, played ball, tag, red rover, and more. We argued and conspired, collaborated and compromised, negotiated and celebrated. We played with army men and little cars in the dirt, made cities, roads, build stick bridges, had miniature wars. Speaking of wars, one of our favorite games was called war. We split up into two sides and chased each other around with toy guns and throwing dirt clod grenades. It was like violent hide and seek and we had arguments about who killed who. We also ran through sprinklers, and swam at the town pool or local lakes. We only went inside to eat or get a drink, although we could easily get a drink from someone's hose. Many of the children I have worked with over the years as an educator don't have these kinds of activities at home for a variety of reasons. Some live in unsafe neighborhoods and have to stay inside all the time. More and more parents are giving into their fears, even when the neighborhoods are safe, and not allowing children unsupervised time outside. And then we cut back on their free play time at school as well.

Some Saturdays I went to the YMCA. We swam, played in the gym, ate snacks and in one of the rooms downstairs they set up a 16mm projector and showed serial films. Serial films used to be shown in the movie theaters before TV. They were short films that told a story in short segments and then you had to come back next week to see the next part. I remember one serial that was about the good sailors in the tropics somewhere, fighting pirates. At the end of each part the hero would face some disaster, but he would always escape. In one episode he was locked in a box that was then smashed by a huge stone. The next week it was revealed that he had rolled out of a hidden trap door in the box just before the smashing took place.

Holidays we spent with family. Thanksgiving meant all my nieces and nephews and brothers and sisters and brother-in-laws and sister-in-laws and grandparents would arrive and spend the day at our house. Two nephews and one niece were older than me and the rest were very close in age, so that was always a lot of fun to run and play with them and all the smells of the food cooking. Christmas likewise, the family came to visit sometimes all at once, sometimes in pieces. In the summer we had my mother's family reunion. The Rosses were a huge clan.

My mom had 10 brothers and sisters, two sets of twins. My mom was one of the younger ones and a twin herself. Her oldest brother Keith was killed in WW I at the Battle of Belleau Wood. Her twin Carl (who I am named after) was killed in WWII lost at sea where he served in the merchant marines. They gathered (and actually still gather) in Aurora Indiana where my mom grew up. She lived most of her life in a little house just up the hill from the park on Park Avenue. My dad's father died when my dad was 3 years old, so we didn't know much about his side of the family. My dad's mother remarried and we spent time with Ma and Pa at their house in Connersville Indiana. Later on after Ma died, Pa came to live with us for a while.

I never realized how much learning came from my family and all of these gatherings. I learned from all of them and from the people I met and interacted with all my life.

School now, school was a whole different animal. It was totally separate from everything else. Long weary days of toil broken up by recess and days and weeks off. I can really only remember snapshots of school as I grew up.

In Kindergarten all I can remember is a Christmas program where all the kindergartners had cardboard Christmas trees to hold in front of us as we sang a song at the Christmas show at Jefferson Elementary School in Lima Ohio. We have old home movies of me with my cardboard tree acting silly. I have a vivid memory of a performance or practice in front of the school body. Shortly before we were to leave the classroom to go to the auditorium/gym to perform I asked to use the restroom. When I returned to the classroom my classmates and teacher were gone. I looked for them and finally found them performing our song in the auditorium. When I finally was reunited with my class my teacher said I had to go out and sing the song by myself. She may have been joking or irritated with me, but I will never forget the terror I felt about performing solo in front of the school which either didn't happen or I blocked the memory. Later on in life I came to love to perform as an actor and musician.

We lived across the street from Jefferson Elementary School and we got an hour for lunch. The school did not serve hot lunches so every day I would walk home and hurriedly eat and then run outside to play with my best friends and next door neighbors John and Jim Winget.

In first grade I was in a split class with my friend John Winget who was in second grade. The teacher taught two separate lessons and I imagine I learned a few things listening to the second grade instruction.

For second grade my family moved across town and I went to I Horace Mann Elementary. Horace Mann actually consisted of two buildings. The "new" building had lower grades and the "old" building which seemed quite ancient to me contained upper grades. My memories of second grade had to do with being nervous about lunch in the cafeteria and reminding my teacher several times every morning that I had packed my lunch. I think I was afraid that someone would make me eat the school lunch.

Third grade moved me to the "old" building and a brand new first year teacher Miss McAlpin. We had a lot of fun that year. I remember making a play that had to do with a train and cardboard boxes. Often, when new teachers enter the profession they are thrown into the deep end of the pool with little mentoring or coaching and expected to learn how to swim. I think there were days we made our new teacher sorry that she had entered the profession. We liked her but we were rowdy.

For fourth grade I had Mrs. Gray, a very old teacher who was quite nearsighted. That year the boys who sat in the back of the class somehow made a game with pieces of notebook paper folded into tanks, jeeps, airplanes and soldiers. We warred with each other behind schoolbooks propped up to look like we were doing something academic. I also remember boys sneaking out of the room to go down to the basement restrooms to play and Mrs. Gray coming after us with a paddle.

Fifth grade is a blank except that it marked the end of the "old" building. Over the summer they tore it down and built a brand new junior high.

West Junior High housed my sixth grade class. Mrs. Holl was the teacher and I remember a parent teacher conference in which she told my parents that I was not taking things seriously and I needed to work harder.

My elementary years were marked with boredom, fun, math that was hard to figure out sometimes (with seemingly endless repetitions), a loathing of round-robin reading which I stupidly used as a beginning teacher, a love of books, writing, and playing with my friends, crushes on girls, fights with friends (not too many - I gave John Fox a bloody nose once and had an aversion to fighting after that), and a variety of teachers who did their best to motivate and instruct me, but who had no more idea than I did about what I needed to prepare for my adolescent and adult life.

It is somewhat amazing, but maybe not too surprising that I remember little of what I learned in elementary school. Times tables, long division, and some distorted mishmash of history.

7th grade at West Junior High meant switching classes, starting band, and beginning to feel more grown up. The new building housed 7th - 9th grades. I found my old report cards a while back so I know I had classes in Health/Science, Industrial Arts, Physical Education, Math, Geography, Art, and English, but I don't remember much about any of them. Apparently I was more adept at English and Geography than Math because I got better grades. I did get paddled once in 7th grade. Pat Hammond and I were having a pen fight in Science class and Mr. Pope took us out in the hall and gave us each a swat on the rear. Teachers and principals did that routinely back then. Not sure it did anything to quell the chronic behavior problems but it scared us timid kids.

1970 and I was in 8th grade. The school system must have invested in computers because the progress reports were printed on the paper that has the holes on each side. Even though I finished 7th grade with a C- in Math I was placed in Advanced Math in 8th grade. I also had band, PE, English, History, Art, and Industrial Arts. My History teacher was a cool guy named Mr. Wilson. Mr. Wilson started a teen club downtown that made a big impact on my life. I helped clean up and paint the rooms that were upstairs in the business district. He was also the manager of a high school rock band. Something about him inspired me but again the details are fuzzy. I liked being in his class and I looked up to him outside of class. In 9th grade my friend Fritz and I wrote an underground school newspaper (mimeographed at local synagogue) called the Underground Railroad and sold it for 10 cents across the street from the school. I got called into the principal's office for that one but I don't remember if there was a consequence or not.

Can you relate to the fact that a lot of the creative fun things I did were outside the boundaries of school and sometimes resulted in some disciplinary action?

For 10th grade they moved us to the high school which was in the center of town. I usually got a ride to school from my buddy Dave Moser's dad who lived behind us. After school I usually walked home. It was about a 2 mile walk. The Lima schools did not bus anyone (at least that I remember) so you either got a ride or walked. I got a driver's license when I was 16, but never owned a car until after high school.

My sophomore year was marked with racial unrest. I remember black kids running down the hall banging on doors and lockers. Somewhere in there we got a new principal Fred Moore who tried to unify the student body. I was into drama and acted in "To Be Young, Gifted, and Black" by Lorraine Hansbury with some of my black classmates. I was in many plays in high school. Karan Longbrake, the drama teacher, had a big impact on me.

It was the liberal 70's so I took a lot of classes I liked and left out most math and science classes. I took all the drama classes I could (some of them more than once), creative writing, typing (I felt this was necessary to become a writer), literature, and art. I also learned how to work the system. If there were classes I didn't feel like attending I would skip homeroom so I would end up on the absence list and then change the dates on previous absence slips so I could attend classes that I wanted to go to and skip the ones I didn't want to go to. I was on "stage crew" so had access to hiding places backstage including several small rooms where we had set up complicated board games like "Axis and Allies", a WWII simulation. We would sneak out of the side door and go to lunch at one of the local burger joints in someone's car.

So I managed to run my own program under the radar at high school. I assume I was in a small minority as most either followed the prescribed path or got kicked out. I had a lot of fun in high school and made a lot of friends. Dave Mason and I used to stand on the shelves in art class and hide behind the heavy drapes on the windows and make bird noises. The art teacher, Mrs. Brown, always laughed and called us her "bats in the belfry". I was "Mr. Drama" and wanted to go on to a career as a writer and actor. Life got in the way of those things as I became a father before shortly after I graduated from high school. Of course few "actors/writers" ever make a living at those pursuits, especially with a wife and baby.

I married Pam in June 1975, also the month I graduated from high school. I was accepted at Blackburn College in Carlinville, Illinois as a theater major. Crystal Dawn was born in October of 1975. I left college in the fall of 1976, because it was becoming impossible to support my family and pay for college working as a gas station attendant. I went to work back in Ohio for a chain of newspapers, and then worked as an insurance salesman for Metropolitan Life. Amber Elizabeth was born in October of 1977. Somewhere in there I went to work for the family business in paper collectibles. I wasn't happy selling stamps, postcards and books to people. I was looking for something with more meaning. I read a book called *36 Children* by Herb Kohl about his experiences teaching a class of 6th graders in Harlem and I realized that I wanted to become a teacher. I quit the family business, enrolled at The Ohio State University Lima branch and went to work at the YMCA youth department.

At Ohio State I discovered a love for analyzing literature that I had never known before. John

Hellman, English professor, taught several fascinating courses. I took his Shakespeare course, a course he taught about film director Alfred Hitchcock, and one called Film and Literature that compared various novels and stories to films (not necessarily based on the books or stories). He opened my eyes to a world of symbolism and metaphor that I had never known about before. I made a short film for one of my education classes about B.F. Skinner and classroom management systems based on his ideas. I also did an independent study in art and filmmaking.

I got divorced from my first wife in 1982. I met my current wife Robin in 1985, although we waited until 1991 to get married. My son Nicholas was born in 1985 and Bryan was born in 1987. In 1988 I did student teaching at Westwood Elementary School in Lima in sixth grade. The teacher stayed around for a couple of days and then I was on my own. It was fun but terrifying. I think I had 30 sixth graders including one of my future son-in-laws. We made a movie that spring about school fighting. I graduated with a bachelor's degree in elementary education and starting substitute teaching in Ohio. In 1989 I was hired as a teacher by Elkhart Community schools

I began teaching second grade, taking over in January for a retiring teacher. I relied heavily on my second grade colleagues and their worksheet approach (for mere survival). We also did read alouds and more. There is a kind of terror a teacher faces when they enter a classroom full of children. The fear is that if you don't keep them busy they will run wild and you will lose your job, not to mention your sanity. So we kept busy. Poor kids. I was probably one of the worst second grade teachers in history!

The next year I taught sixth grade in a portable classroom because the school had become overcrowded. We had the advantage of air conditioning when it was hot, but the disadvantage of having to go into the school building for restrooms, lunch, specials like gym, art, music etc, and a long walk to the office if I had a phone call or if I needed to make a phone call or make copies. That year I knocked some boys off the football team due to grades and then was told by the principal that I had to use the basal reader instead of my whole language books. The next year because of changes in the school enrollment numbers and my lack of seniority I was moved to Mary Feeser Elementary School just down the road. I spent the next 25 years there as a teacher and assistant principal.

I taught sixth grade for the majority of my career, taught fourth twice and fifth once. After 17 years in the classroom I became an administrator and was assistant principal for 8 years before being placed in charge of elementary alternative for my school system. A couple of those years I experimented with what I called IWP's, individual work plans. I broke sixth grade standards down into numbered lists and let students work at their own pace. I still did some instructional episodes during the day, but during independent work time, they worked on their own iwp at their own pace. It was an interesting but flawed experiment. Some students finished quickly and some were very slow (which was kind of the idea) which led to problems with record keeping and also what to do at the end of the year when they hadn't done all of the standards. I will address standards in greater detail later in this book.

I was an odd teacher. The Ohio State University was famous at the time for promoting "Whole Language" approach to reading which favored whole books over basal readers, and downplayed the instruction of phonics and other more mechanical approaches to reading instruction. Teacher Ed had also promoted experiential math instruction which involved introducing concepts to students with the use of cooperative learning and manipulatives instead of textbook and worksheets. After I settled in and found my feet I would often do what I thought of as cool and fun things in class. We did plays, movies, songs, and more. One year during the last quarter of the year we ran our own TV station with news shows, dramas, etc. What I didn't think about at the time was how little room I left for the student's to develop their own interests. Everything was always based on what I thought was "cool and fun". Some of them loved parts of it, but no matter what I did somebody was left out.

At some point I came up with the idea of a social studies game as a way to help students better understand history, social systems, and different forms of government. The way the game worked is that we created our own world called "Terra Portiba" after our portable classroom. Each person had a character that they created giving them numbers for different attributes. This game was partially based on "Dungeons and Dragons" where people create fantasy characters and then sit around a table talking and rolling dice to find out outcomes. After kids made their characters I had them write down what they wanted to do on papers we called, "interactions". My thought here was to encourage them to do more writing and to try to think logically using techniques and resources we were reading about in the social studies book. Some kids loved writing interactions and creating tools, houses, etc for their characters and some kids hated it and it was like pulling teeth to get them to write interactions. We started with Stone Age characters and moved through different periods of history including ancient Greece and Rome, the Middle Ages, etc. Some of the boys loved battling, the system for which I stole from the board game Risk. We would roll up to six dice against six dice of the other army and you could lose that many soldiers. Anyway, this is an example of a "cool and fun" activity that some students lived for and others couldn't stand, didn't like and didn't want to do.

We also did a film that was our version of "The Wizard of Oz", complete with Dorothy, the Wicked Witch, and munchkins, wrote songs and made music videos. We wrote poetry, and plays and stories. We had a daily sharing time. I will never forget the day one of our (I thought) quiet, reserved girls did a hootchie cootchie dance which had me breathless from laughter.

I was never big on worksheets. We read books and wrote in journals. Every day kids were supposed to write words from their reading that they either didn't know or found interesting. On Monday I asked random kids to supply a word from their journals and we made a list of 20. We would write a meaning and then the "spelling" test which I renamed "vocabulary" consisted of me saying a word and kids writing it in a sentence spelling it correctly and showing that they knew the meaning.

All these practices were my way of making school more real and meaningful, but notice where the control was - all with me, the adult.

I got my Master's degree from Indiana Wesleyan and then decided to get my administrator's license. I felt that I had been able to affect some children's lives in a positive way as a teacher and I thought I could help more kids as a principal so after 17 years as a classroom teacher I became an administrator. The first year I team taught with Amy Petersen. I taught in the morning and then spent the afternoon as "administrative assistant". After that year I became the assistant principal. As part of that job I worked with kids of all ages who were struggling with "behavior". I learned a little bit about what causes misbehavior.

At school we try to figure out what is causing "misbehavior". We seek to find the function of the behavior with the idea that humans don't engage in behavior for no reasons unless they are severely mentally ill. Often we think that students act out because of a need for attention combined with avoiding certain situations. So say a kid doesn't like math and doesn't feel successful at math. They quickly find out that they can attract attention during math in a way that disguises the fact that they can't do it and gets them kicked out so they achieve two things at once. They receive positive or negative attention for being cool, or being funny, or being a troublemaker, and they avoid the hated math work. Also sometimes the kid has some growing to do or has some mental health issues, but many times the problems come because of the way school is organized. So what if we don't make the kid do math? Hmmmm, maybe the behavior would go away because the need for avoidance would no longer exist. We might still have to deal with the need for attention, but that is an easier problem to deal with when everyone is engaged in doing what they want to do. More about that later.

I spent 7 years as assistant principal, worked well with Kevin Dean, the principal. I was able to have an impact on many issues that I care about including classroom management, student/adult relationships, and grading practices. During that time our superintendent retired and the new leader, Rob Haworth, wanted to give each building that had an older principal a younger assistant so they could be groomed to eventually take over the building. Since Kevin and I are about the same age, I was going to be moved. I met with Dr. Haworth to talk about options and he brought up alternative programs. I had always had a heart for kids who struggled with school so I jumped at the chance and started doing some research into alternative programs.

Historically in Elkhart alternative placements are based on behavior. If a student is not functioning well in the traditional behavior system, a building is supposed to put interventions into place including rewards, punishments, instruction, alteration of schedule or length of day, etc. If these interventions do not result in compliance, then other interventions may be tried, but eventually a student may be considered for alternative placement. In the past, alternative placement has meant a full or half day program in a different location, trying many of the same interventions in a more intense way with more adults around to help children comply. After I worked with this system for a year and a half, I found there were some kids that weren't too interested in complying. I began to wonder if maybe the adults were more of the problem than the children.

One of the reasons I began to believe adults were more of the problem was the reluctance classroom teachers and building administrators had to changing their practices. I was frustrated because it seems like we have known for a while that certain ways of instructing are at best ineffective and at worst actually have a negative impact on learning. Endless worksheets, round robin reading, taking away recess, yelling, harsh grading practices are examples of practices that don't work and can make children hate school. But when I would bring up doing something different I was often met with sullen resentment or outright anger. Something as simple as using choral response to a question instead of calling on kids who had their hands raised seemed to offend some teachers.

As I became aware of students who were being suspended because of behavior and even put on "homebound" instruction I began to look for other ways to keep kids in the learning loop. Homebound instruction is when a kid sits at home and a teacher arranges to meet with them several times a week. They do work together and then the teacher assigns work to do before the next meeting. We are allowed to count this as full time instruction because the student is under the direction of a certified teacher. A friend of mine, Gary McAllister who used to teach 6th grade next door to me, was working at the local science education nonprofit called Ethos. They offered hands-on science classes to home school kids. Twice a week for 2 hours at a time, retired teachers worked with kids to explore different science topics. Cooperative learning, small groups, non-coercive environment and methods were the norm for these classes. They were also very hands on. I got the bright idea to send some of homebound and alternative kids to the ETHOS classes. Over a period of a year, we sent 6 kids to ETHOS who were not making it in their elementary classes and the amazing thing is that many of the issues they were having at school disappeared. This further reinforced the idea that the problem was the system and the adults, more than the children.

We also launched an alternative program at 3 elementary schools based on a program that I had discovered in Marion Indiana. We designed the program to modify children's behavior and teach skills needed to be successful in traditional school. When children entered the program they would work their way through levels until they showed the ability to comply and follow rules so that they could go back to the regular classroom. It worked for some kids, but we found that there were some that it didn't work for. Some children seemed to prefer to be in the alternative room. We theorized that this could be because of several factors: 1. We worked hard to build relationships with kids. 2. It was usually quiet and peaceful in the alternative room. 3. We encouraged kids to do work but we didn't yell or scream if they didn't. If they engaged in passive resistance or went to sleep, we didn't bother them, figuring that it just slowed down their transition back to their regular class, but wasn't really hurting anyone. 4. Some of them didn't like their teacher or their class so there was little motivation to work towards going back.

The other outcome of our relationship with ETHOS was that I became more aware of home school families. In Indiana any parent can choose to home school their children. Some of those choose home school due to religious beliefs. Some feel that schools are too lax or don't meet their children's needs. Some kids are victims of bullying, so parents decide to keep them at home. I spent some time talking to home school parents and watching the home school kids and often they seemed to have the same issues our behavior kids had. I began to wonder if there was a way to help any kid who didn't fit traditional school. I reached out to some home school parents via email and one of them responded and asked me if I had heard of self-directed learning and Dr. Peter Gray. I immediately looked him up and ordered his book *Free to Learn*. It is an amazing book that everyone who cares about children should read. I will reference it a lot throughout this book. It opened my eyes to many things, not the least of which is that we need to drastically change how we do school. Through that book and other places I became aware of Sudbury Valley School in Framingham Massachusetts, a school that has been in existence since 1968. At SVS they allow students total freedom to choose their educational path. I ordered a planning kit and read books, listened to cds, and watched DVDs and became more and more convinced that I had stumbled on the way school should be done and would be done in the future.

Around the same time I had read a book called *Disrupting Class* which explored the way that disruption has caused revolutionary changes in social and economic institutions and how those same forces are already at work in destroying the educational monolithic authoritarian system. Disruptive change can occur when a certain sector of the market is dominated by a monolithic organization that is resistant to change. A competitor enters the market serving neglected segments of the population and very quickly can become dominant and all but put the established company out of business. Examples include IBM's dominance in the computer world until upstarts Apple and Microsoft came along and took over, and how film cameras gave way to digital. The book says that a similar revolution is on the horizon for education. The current monolithic public school system is very resistant to change and outliers are already taking away customers. Estimates are that 2 million children are experiencing some form of homeschooling. There are also hundreds of schools that operate on a spectrum of freedom from totally free to adult controlled schools that are more child-friendly but not really free.

I dreamed of a public school where students would have freedom in almost every way including times to come in and leave, what to study and when, and the freedom to play and enjoy life. In the spring of 2017 Dana Irving and I and 12 children embarked on an experiment to see if we could allow students to choose how to spend their day. We developed 10 guiding principles that we refined and improved as we went along.

1. People have the right to pose their own questions and seek their own answers.
2. People have the right to seek help from others.
3. People have the right to be safe.
4. People have the right to play and enjoy life.
5. People have the right to a stimulating environment with many different learning tools, opportunities, and inspirations.
6. People have the right to politely say no, unless they are unsafe or bothering other people.
7. People have the right to express their thoughts, hopes, fears, dreams, and needs in a polite and respectful way.

8. People have the responsibility to listen to and respect others.
9. People have the responsibility to make smart choices and admit when they make mistakes.
10. People have the responsibility to abide by the rules that have been established for the safety and comfort of the group.

We were given a classroom in an existing elementary school - smack in the middle of it, which proved to be a problem. We began on April 26 and had six weeks to sink or swim. We were also given the use of a 14 passenger bus which we used to pick up students in the morning at 3 schools and then return them at the end of the day, and also to go on field trips. Some of our students were dropped off by parents and one came on a regular school bus. We took most of the desks out of the room and got a sofa and a bunch of cushions, and a beanbag chair. We would usually arrive at school by 9 or so, kids would have breakfast. Some of them would go to sleep; some would get on the two desktop computers, four ipads, or 2 chromebooks. We developed a sign up list on the dry erase board and would draw student cards and asked them what they wanted to do.

Some would choose legos or to play with toys. Some had their own devices or phones.

Some days we would stay at school all day. We could go outside when the other students weren't out or we could go to the tennis courts or woods behind the playground. There was also a public park right across the street from the school that we would sometimes drive the bus to. We took many excursions to other parks, to an animal shelter in nearby South Bend, to Ethos Science Center, and a few local restaurants.

The first few weeks were very difficult. Students picked at each other over trivial matters, cursed at each other, fought sometimes, and ran out of the room and out of the school. One of our most difficult girls moved away and we had to put one boy on homebound because he just couldn't seem to handle the freedom. At about week 4 partly because of the two departures and partly because the other kids were getting more used to the philosophy, it felt like the program was calming down and beginning to work. We still had rough days, but we saw many glimmers of success. Dana and I realized that children would need a "detox" period to work out some of their personal issues. We saw students being kinder to each other, working together more, and beginning to work on some interesting projects. About the time we felt like it was really coming together it was time for summer vacation.

This was our "pilot" program and we learned a lot from it. One of the biggest lessons we learned is that often adults have to let the children work out their disagreements and the solutions they came up with worked better than any we would impose on them. Also we learned that incidents that we thought were major issues were quickly forgotten by the children and therefore resolved by putting it behind them quickly. Kids that were dire enemies one hour were working together and friends the next hour. Often the best thing adults can do is get out of the way and let children figure it out for themselves. A third big lesson we learned is that it is not good to put an alternative program in the middle of an elementary school. We were hoping going forward that we wouldn't have to share spaces with anyone. There are just too many ways we have to tiptoe around the authoritarian structure, too much peace and quiet that we can't disturb, too many rules that don't connect with reality that we have to consider, and too many toes to step on.

Throughout the spring we were planning for next year. I had approached a couple of local churches about the possibility of using their Sunday school spaces for our new school. At first this looked promising but then our school corporation's operations department determined that it would cost too much in security and food service required infrastructure changes to make that idea feasible. We then thought we had found an ideal location. The school corporation actually owned a house adjacent to one of the elementary buildings. Again that idea was vetoed because of the cost of upgrading.

We finished the school year not knowing where we would be housed the next year. We had a commitment to the program and staffing with one administrator/teacher (me), a second teacher, and 3 academic trainers. Our list of children originally had 36 names on it, including 10 from our pilot program, which we whittled down to 24 and then to 20 by the time school started.

In late July we were notified that we would be housed at Pierre Moran Middle School. At first I was dismayed by the prospect of being in a middle school. For one thing I really wanted to be in a space that was all ours that we didn't share with anyone. We were to be given two classrooms. My fear was that they would be small, non-connected, and not close to an exit. The exit was important because we wanted students to be able to go outside any time they wanted to and a nearby exit would make that convenient and less disruptive to our host school.

I arranged to meet with Cindy Bonner, the middle school principal, to see where our space would be and was very pleasantly surprised and in awe at her generosity. She was going to allow us to use the old technical education classroom and lab, so instead of two small classrooms, we had a very large room which we came to call the "front room" and a 32 unit computer lab, plus 3 other small rooms. The space was perfect for us and very close to an exit that we could use as our own dedicated entrance as well. In August we began the work of cleaning out the rooms and getting ready for students.

For our staff we had Dana Irving who had embarked on our pilot program with me and had run one of our classrooms at Roosevelt Steam Academy, and Tabitha Olinger who had come on board at our classroom at Osolo in January of 2017 and had worked previously at an alternative school in Warsaw Indiana. We were losing our trainer from Beck Elementary School, but we managed to get Tammie Thompson formerly our Beck trainer to come in as a long-term sub. We were also fortunate enough to hire Nanci Tarantino as our teacher. She came to us from a residential psychiatric facility and was looking for a job in an alternative setting. In November we finally completed our team with David Cassell who had previously worked at the Civil Rights Center at the South Bend IUSB campus. We also shared a behavior specialist with the alternative program for older students. Jason Miller began the year but then left and in December we hired Kerry Guernsey.

We managed to do some training in the spring and summer and went over the philosophy and expectations of the program, but no matter how much talking and training you do, it is not real until the children arrive.

We began on August 17 with 20 children. Again, the beginning was difficult. The kids seemed wild. They weren't nice to each other or us. They ran around. They ran out. They cursed. They fought. They yelled. Some days and some weeks at the beginning we were despairing, afraid that we had made a huge mistake, that these kids would never be able to handle freedom and responsibility. But then, after a while, it got better. We had our ups and downs, but overall it felt like we were making progress. By late November, early December we noticed some changes occurring. The children were less apt to fight. They were more likely to work out issues, not always kindly, but with words instead of fists. There was more time to talk to them, especially the quiet ones, and they were more open to doing some academic work.

In September we had given an NWEA test which is a standardized test that shows if a child is progressing in their learning. We repeated it in December and most of our students improved and some of them hit their spring targets in winter. We found this remarkable because we hadn't really done any organized classes. Learning took place because students were interacting with each other, playing games on the computer and off, going outside, negotiating with each other and us when they needed something and doing some online learning through watching videos or through mobymax online learning system. Nanci and I sometimes were able to pull kids aside and do a little reading or math with them, but many of them refused even this little piece of instruction. In May we gave the tests again. 19 out of 22 improved in Reading and 18 out of 22 improved in Math. We also beat the average growth. Not that everyone was "on grade level", just that they improved.

At the beginning of year 2 we weren't sure what to expect. We started with 13 children and quickly added others. We were amazed when we were able to add a morning meeting in September which we called "Team Time" that students were able to sit down and listen to each other and vote on important matters that came up from time to time.

Overall, individually and for our program, we have seen tremendous growth in learning and social skills. Kid's ability to reason, talk, negotiate, explain and communicate has grown by leaps and bounds.

Working in an environment of freedom is scary, exciting, wonderful, and difficult. The adults and children have embarked on a journey. None of us know where it will end, but it is changing us and will continue to change us forever. We learn new things every day. Most days all of us show up which in itself is a testament to the program. Children don't want to go at the end of the day. The staff comes early and stays late. I can't imagine ever going back to the way I used do school and I hope that anyone who reads this book will join us and start looking for ways to institute the changes I am going to suggest in the rest of the chapters at any school you have any influence over. Whether you are a teacher, parent, grandparent, clergyperson, aid, young person, or just a concerned citizen, get involved with your schools. Ask them why they do things the way they do them and keep asking. Suggest some of the ideas I have included in this book or in other books or videos and see if we can slowly move this titanic institution called public education into a better sea lane before it hits the inevitable iceberg.

Chapter 2 - Should children be grouped by age in grade levels?

First day of Kindergarten a bunch of 5 year olds enter school. Keonte likes to color and write his letters. He can count to 20 and knows many words. His parents have always read aloud to him and he has several books memorized. Samantha knows no letters, can't count, can't tie her shoes, and is not sure of her own name. Throw in 20 more all scattered across the continuum of what they know and can do. Mr. Kelly a new teacher is at a loss of how to help all the children.

Once upon a time there was a group of 30 year olds who were grouped together by the government randomly. One was a waiter at a fancy restaurant, one was a cop, one was a doctor, one was a lawyer, one worked at home, one was a drug dealer, and on and on - a variety of people in a variety of occupations - all the same age 25 total. One day the group leader announced that the next day they were taking a trip to Detroit, Michigan free to all. They would pursue all kinds of interesting and fun activities, museums, the riverfront, maybe a sporting event and of course good food to eat. Was the group thrilled about the idea? How would you react if you were a part of the group? What would the pluses and minuses be?

The reactions of the group were varied: some liked the idea, some hated it, some had other plans, some had obligations, and some were not interested in Detroit or in any of the "fun activities". In addition the members of the group were scattered all over the area - as far as 100 miles away.

This is what happens in traditional school all the time. Just because of age we try to force kids to go on learning journeys to the same destination, no matter what they think or what their abilities or interests are.

Besides convenience is there really any good reason to group children by age? There are even definite advantages to multi age groupings. I think we can approach the answers through logic and common sense as well as research.

If you observe groups of children do they naturally divide themselves up by age? Sometimes they seek out children about the same age, but often they may be looking for other children who have the same interests or similar abilities. At times they may look for someone who knows how to do something that they want to learn to do so they can observe or just ask questions.

Why do we group children by age? Part of the justification comes from the idea that there are certain topics or standards that need to be taught and learned at a certain age. This brings its own bag of troubles which I will address in another chapter. If you accept the idea that certain standards need to be learned by a certain age then you would be trapped with the grade level system we have now. But if you think about what we know about how human beings learn you may come to the conclusion that the idea of standards is ridiculous. Every person is an individual and learns at their own pace. Not everyone is interested in the same thing at the same time as everyone else. We know from brain research that true learning comes from the interests of the learner.

When children enter Kindergarten at about age 5 it is amazing to see the variety in what they already know and what they can and cannot do. Immediately at school we try to corral them and force them to learn the curriculum. Right away we run into trouble. Some of these kids already know the alphabet, letter sounds, and numbers. Some can already tie their shoes, zip up their pants, and hold a pencil. Some may even be reading already. Others don't know their own name, only know some letters, and are not able to count. Some may not even be talking in sentences. In too many schools 5 year olds are confined to their seats for extended periods of time. Young children by nature are active, inquisitive, curious, and looking for fun. Too many of them quickly find out that school is not fun. Some children find themselves immediately labeled as failures. We teach them right away that school is hard boring work and if they are not instantly good at it, we bear down harder on them. School staff and parents start to panic if they don't make immediate progress in math and reading. What if some children just need more time to be ready to learn these things? They may need more time to explore, play, and develop other talents.

By about January schools start to think about retaining students in Kindergarten. Retention has not had much support in research as an effective remediation tool. But the only alternative in many cases is to just send the kids to first grade where they may be made to feel even more failure because they have not learned all the skills that are prerequisite to learning the new things in first grade. The age/grade level system compounds this every year and every year teachers and parents face the same dilemma: retain the student or pass them on. What if there were no grade levels? What if students could pursue interests at their own pace? What if they had older children that could help them in ways adults can't?

If we abolish grade levels then children could move at their pace based on their interests. That also clears the way for them to shoot ahead if and when they become interested in something. Often traditional classes are taught to the middle of the group. Those who are behind are bored and frustrated because they don't understand what is being taught and quickly lose any interest in the subject. Those who are ahead of the group are bored and frustrated because they are listening to something that they already know and unless the teacher is skillful enough to give them more interesting work they also lose interest and may even question why they are forced to attend the class.

Here is how the ILEAD School in California extols the virtues of multi age education, "Multi-age education is an approach to teaching and learning that truly allows the academic and social-emotional needs of every learner to be met. In multi-age environments, learners are able to work on skills and concepts that are appropriate based on where they fall in the learning continuum, regardless of their age. In the meantime, social interaction among older and younger learners promotes leadership and positive social-emotional behaviors. Older learners may model problem-solving and communication skills for their younger peers and vice versa."

In Indiana the state legislature passed a law that all third grade students must take a reading test called IREAD 3. If they don't pass the test in early March they will have another opportunity in June. If they still fail to pass they will be retained in 3rd grade. Later they revised the rule to say they could be designated as 4th graders but would need to receive 3rd grade reading instruction and would have to take IREAD test again. The law said they could be retained twice if they failed to pass the test. Imagine what that does to the self-esteem of the child! It also creates situations where schools have students who turn 14 during their sixth grade year. Studies also show that one of the biggest predictors of a student dropping out of high school is a previous retention. The percentage goes up for students who have been retained twice.

The flip side of this is that if you really believe that students need to learn certain concepts and attain specific skills by a certain age, what do you do with the ones who don't? We could retain them in the grade until they master the material - but do we want 16 year olds in first grade? A different kind of multi-age but clearly absurd.

If there are no grade levels the impact of IREAD and other tests is diminished. For students in the alternative program I helped create and run, it would make absolutely no difference in their daily routine whether they pass the test or not. A lot of research shows that when students feel less pressure to perform they actually do better on thinking tasks. So you may do better on a test if you don't perceive it as high stakes.

Some studies exist that seem to indicate that students in multiage settings perform better on standardized tests, have fewer problems with behavior, and benefit socially. Problems with the approach appear to be mostly logistical.

One benefit to multi-age groupings noted by several authors including Peter Gray are that younger students look up to older students and may actually learn more from children 2-3 years older than themselves than they do from adults. Older students actually become more empathetic and have more compassion when they experience helping younger students. Examples in books by Daniel Greenburg (Sudbury Valley School) and Gray relate how younger students watch older students do something and were inspired to try it themselves. This could range from walking up a slide to reading big thick books. I have seen this myself in our program. Some of our learners love to ride bikes at a nearby skate park and some of the younger ones watch the older ones do tricks on the bike and then try it themselves. In a few cases older students try to teach younger ones how to perform a trick. We also see this when they do tumbling. Some of the older students can do front and back flips and the younger ones are inspired to try it also.

In schools such as Sudbury Valley School in Framingham Massachusetts, students from age 4 to 19 spend their time associating with whoever they choose. Students often associate with students more than 2 years older or younger than themselves. Graduates report that they were inspired to learn to read because they saw the older students reading and discussing what they read.

Studies of children that were in mixed age situations have shown that older children can raise the level of sociodramatic play by introducing ideas and concepts that the younger children would not think of on their own.

In *Free to Learn* Peter Gray writes: "Part of the natural process of growing up is to look ahead, at those who are further along but not so far ahead as to be out of reach. Five-year-olds aren't particularly interested in emulating adults, who are too much in a different world. But five-year-olds do very much want to be like the cool eight- and nine-year-olds they see around them. If those eight- and nine-year-olds are reading and discussing books, or playing computer games, or climbing trees, or collecting Magic the Gathering cards, then the five-year-olds want to do that too. Similarly, eight- and nine-year-olds look to young teens as models; young teens look to older teens; and older teens look to adults. This all occurs naturally in an age-mixed environment such as Sudbury Valley. People don't have to establish themselves deliberately as role models for younger children; they simply are."

David Lancy is an anthropologist who has studied children in many different cultures. He wrote in the book *The Anthropology of Learning in Childhood*, "The single most important form of learning is observation." In many traditional cultures learning is accomplished by children observing and imitating their elders. Yet in our traditional schools we tell children that they must work on their own and not copy others. The only expert in a traditional classroom is the teacher. What if a child had a mixture of experts of differing levels to observe and copy?

Another advantage of mixing ages is that students can spend more than one year with the same adult staff members. In traditional schools you would normally change teachers each year.

I once had an opportunity to do a 3 year loop with the same core group of students. It was interesting starting the second year and students not having to relearn all the procedures and quirks of a teacher. It also allowed me to get to know students better and for them to get to know me better. In our current program we have 5 adults with 20 children, some of whom have been with us for 2 years now. In traditional schools it sometimes feels like you just get to know students and then they move on to someone else. I have often encouraged principals to consider taking their Kindergarten and first grade children and treat them as one big group and then have the teachers regrouping them all the time by interest, ability, and learning style. Children would benefit from the age mixing and it would mean that these kids could also spend more than one year with the same group of adults and form deeper relationships. This seems like a minor step to take without making any radical changes in the physical school, or the schedule, but I could never get anyone to try it. A more revolutionary change would be to let children choose what adults and other children they would like to associate with. Some teachers might have to make some changes if they found no one coming to their class.

At Ann Arbor Open School, they group children in 2 year groups after kindergarten, all the way through 8th grade.

There are also advantages to age mixing for older children. Studies have shown that exposure to younger students increase empathy and reduce bullying behavior in older students. As they learn to care for and help younger students they learn to be more caring and compassionate. When teaching situations arise, whether it is playing cards, reading, playing sports, or just talking, older students are forced to think about what they know and find ways to relay information to younger children in a way that makes sense to them. To teach someone something, often means learning more about it yourself.

What about adults? Could free, democratic, self-directed education benefit adults? I think that one paradigm that would be fascinating to try is to open a learning center that was open to all ages, where everyone could pursue their goals with the help of a multi-age community.

Suggestions

What can schools do that could take advantage of the positives of age mixing?

1. Look at grouping current grade levels in two or three year cohorts. Have all the adults involved collaborate on the best ways to group the students by ability and interest.

2. Looks for ways to systematically have grade level teams spend part of the day working with older or younger students.

3. Consider giving children more choice in who they spend their time with. This could include adults and children.

4. Explore the possibility of teachers at different grade levels co-teaching instead of teachers at the same grade level.

Chapter 3 - Should children learn the same thing at the same time?

Elouise is daydreaming again. It is math time and Mr. Marshall is going over adding with regrouping again. So boring! She caught onto the idea the first week it was brought up and now she is bored out of her skull because half the class isn't getting it. Mr. Marshall glances at her sympathetically. At least he doesn't pick on me, she thinks. She doodles on the math worksheet that they all have. It must be a law somewhere that says everybody has to do the same work at the same time even if they already know how to do it. Elouise looks at her friend Lacy who is staring at the ceiling. Lacy can't even remember her basic addition facts so this is just as boring for her. Lacy still counts on her fingers for problems like 6+2, so regrouping isn't making much sense to her at all.

In *The Underachieving School* John Holt writes, "The idea of a "body of knowledge," to be picked up at school and used for the rest of one's life, is nonsense in a world as complicated and rapidly changing as ours."

Is there a body of knowledge that everyone needs to learn before they leave school? Is it necessary that everyone learn the same skills and information as all their peers? Is it even practical to try to figure out what knowledge people should be exposed to in our modern world of massive information and disinformation?

There may have been a time in world history where it may have been possible to accumulate all the knowledge (at least written knowledge) available in the world, but I doubt it. There have definitely been movements to define what knowledge is important and necessary to become a well educated person. These various lists have been highly subjective and open to cultural bias.

Even if we can agree that there are certain basic skills and understandings that are valuable to most if not all citizens of a certain area, that list of skills and understandings would be markedly different for people living in different areas. People who live in the Bahamas probably don't need to understand ice and snow at the same level as someone living in northern Alaska.

So what are some skills that are important and necessary to live in the 21st Century? I would suggest it is important to be able to find things out and communicate effectively with others. It is valuable to have a basic understanding of history. When it comes to math it is important that people can handle money, make a budget, and avoid being cheated. Other professions may require more specific knowledge but there have been many cases where self-confident learners have been able to quickly fill in gaps in knowledge when they are motivated to do so.

The question I want to address in this chapter is not only is there knowledge that needs to be known by all, but also do they need to learn it at the same time as all the other people their same age?

The American Psychological Association website says this, "Just because you have a classroom full of students who are about the same age doesn't mean they are equally ready to learn a particular topic, concept, skill, or idea. It is important for teachers and parents to understand that maturation of the brain influences learning readiness."

Any teacher who has had any experience with children can tell you how frustrating it can be to try to teach a lesson based on standards because some of the children are ready, some are not ready, and some already know it.

Teaching the same thing at the same time is a convenience for adults. How else can we get the standards covered? There is a concept in education that is called "covering an idea, topic or standard". A teacher can claim to "cover" the standards because they presented the concept and assigned work related to the concept. What no one can honestly claim is that "covering" means that anyone learned the concept or is able to apply it in a different situation. It does seem valuable to me to have a course laid out for anyone who is interested in learning about a subject. Some subjects lend themselves to a sequence of learning. One way to look at standards is to see them as steps on the way to reach a goal. When a person is ready to learn about algebra for instance, here are the steps you should follow to reach your goal.

But I believe it is a huge mistake to treat standards as some kind of rigid inflexible measure of what students should know and be able to do at a certain age. No two people at any age are the same or have the same interests or abilities.

Here is an example of a state standard.
Indiana - Grade 4 -

4.RL.3. Compare and contrast the point of view
2 from which different stories are narrated,
including the difference between
first- and third-person narrations.

This is a fourth grade standard. So a fourth grader is 9 or 10 years old. Some of them may be quite capable of understanding point of view - but I know many adults in their advanced years and with college degrees that get confused on this subject. How would a standard like this be approached at a traditional school? Most likely students would be introduced to some rules such as *If the author uses the pronoun "I" in the narration the text is probably written in first person, and if the author uses the pronoun "he, she, or they" the narration is probably written in the third person.* Next students would be assigned to read some passages that are written in different points of view and asked to identify which point of view they were reading, which they may or may not be able to read or be interested in reading. The identifying of the point of view could be done individually or as a group, either written or orally. The adults who design the lesson, either the teacher or a textbook company, would hopefully be careful to include clear examples of the points of view so the children don't get mixed up. But what happens when, in the middle of a third person narration, dialogue pops up in quotation marks, or interior thoughts (perhaps in italics) using the first person pronoun? Won't that be a stumbling block to the students who really want to do well and may over-apply the first person rule? If they mark the passage as third person, they will get reinforcement from the teacher, their confusion invisible. If they mark it as first person, it will be marked incorrect, sometimes with feedback from the teacher as to why it is wrong, which may also increase their confusion.

Wouldn't it be better to let the children enjoy reading and have some discussions? Is it really important for their future lives that fourth graders understand point of view? Isn't it better to just enjoy good books, newspapers, websites, etc?

In *Sherlock Holmes is Wrong* on the Sudbury Valley School website Scott David Gray writes, "The web site for the "Common Core State Standards Initiative" (an Inter-state organization supported by the US Department of Education in concert with State governments) takes *hundreds of pages* simply to present a *summary* of the ideas and facts that children at various grade levels are expected to agree with, memorize and recite back. Various states and local agencies, as well as various private organizations that advise teachers, add more items to be filed away in students' minds during their schooling."

Examine the common core or individual state standards and you will see that Gray is correct. It seems almost impossible that anyone could learn all the material in state standards in their 13 years of school and hard to imagine what good it would do them if they managed it.

At the Beacon Self-Directed Learning Center they have different views of curriculum and learning, "Remove school paradigms, such as grades, testing and other forms of external validation and open wide pathways to intrinsic motivation. What are you good at? What do you love to do? Discover there are many ways to learn: internships, online classes, projects, tutorials, work experiences, self-study. At Beacon we inspire learning, not force it."

So why do we have standards? In one word, fear! Adults are afraid that children will miss some key information that may come back later to haunt them. It is also fueled by international competition when we compare how students do on standardized tests of various kinds from various countries. In our panic we grasp at something concrete that we can put our hands on or wrap our brains around. It is easier to consult a thick book of standards to guide the planning of today's lesson than to trust in the natural process of children educating themselves.

De Ruimte Democratic School in the Netherlands speaks about their curriculum, "We do not work with a preconceived curriculum. As a result, students take on their personal responsibility and have the wheel in their own hands. Together with staff members and teachers they also fulfill all tasks and roles in the school that are normally only in the hands of the adults. This way we create together the form and content of the school. In the Space children learn from their intrinsic motivation."

Another quote from John Holt, "The adults say, "Suppose they don't learn something they will need later?" The time to learn something is *when* you need it; no one can know what he will need to learn in the future; much of the knowledge we will need 20 years from now may not even exist today."

There is no contest between the learning that occurs when a person investigates their world and works on building models of their world in a self-determined way as opposed to a teacher mandating the state standard that everyone must learn. The former has a much better chance of lasting through the years (perhaps dependent on what direction a person takes in their life). The state standard learning has a slim chance of lasting 30 days let alone 30 years.

If you really believe that there are certain skills and concepts that must be learned at a certain age, then the logical implication is that we should retain students in a grade level until they learn it. Research has shown that not only is retention not a good way to help students, it has a negative impact on their future lives. Someone who has been retained in school is more likely to drop out, be incarcerated, and be on public assistance. If they have been retained twice the percentages of negativity are even higher. If we quit worrying about standards we can empower the learner to follow their interests and passions.

The Open School in Irvine California talks about empowerment on their website, "Students have the power to make their ideas a reality. Free from the confines of curriculum, they can procure whatever materials they need using the school's budget, or request instruction either from on-site staff or outside professionals. They can organize field trips to anywhere, from the local arboretum to a distant national park. Students here have the same administrative power as staff. They can be elected to committees and positions of authority. They learn how to be leaders and how to enact change in their communities and beyond."

Mountain Play Place in Irvine California has this to say about curriculum, "Children at Play Mountain learn far more than the "Three R's." They learn to live fully and joyfully in the world, with a deep understanding of who they are, what they are interested in, and a profound respect for others. Students here are creative, self-motivated problem-solvers with an abiding curiosity about the world and, they become equipped with all the tools they will need for a lifetime of continued learning."

Much time is spent in schools and in school corporations worrying and fussing over curriculum. I would say a lot of this is misplaced mental energy. As I said previously about standards, curriculum is useful if it is a kind of guide post to let you know some things that it would be helpful to know and be able to do at certain points in your life. But often in school it is treated as some kind of inviolable law that everyone has to know certain things and that the child, the teachers, and the school have failed if they don't reach those benchmarks by a certain calendar date.

Old or new curriculums can be helpful for different reasons, but knowledge is changing so fast that often even the latest curriculum is woefully out of date by the time it is published.

I don't believe that the failure of schools has anything to do with good or bad curriculum. If your school has healthy, happy children, and healthy, happy adults, just about any curriculum can be a starting point. The key is letting children make decisions for themselves with the help of caring adults.

Suggestions

1. Look at the vertical articulation of standards and determine what the ultimate iteration is. Then look at groups of children and see if you can identify where they are on the range of the standards. Allow them freedom to choose activities that are most interesting to them.
2. Look at the standards as a way to design some learning opportunities to students that they can take or leave alone.
3. Consider allowing learners to choose their own curriculum.

Chapter 4 - Is Play an extra? Is it less important than instruction?

Kasei, aged 8, is standing on a thingamajig twirling around on the playground. She starts talking about how she can cast spells on people. "If I am in a bad mood it could be a bad spell, but if I am in a good mood I might turn you into a unicorn. Unicorns are good and they battle the evil Pegasus. Some of the unicorns lost their horns and grew wings and became evil. Those are the evil Pegasus. They fight each other and the good unicorns always win." I told her that we should write all that down in a book and draw pictures and she said, "No, it is a secret, you can't tell anyone."

Peter Gray, in all his work, but especially in his book, *Free to Learn*, has clearly established that the natural learning tool for all mammals (and many other animals) is play. From birth human beings explore their world and like young scientists experiment with language, movement, and social interactions. They learn a ton of skills and information in their first few years. Children are born seeking information.

Children learn and explore and play. This does not end at any age unless we actively shut it down. Sometimes parents mistakenly do this in the name of getting kids ready for school. Some pre-schools may require a child to sit for extended periods of time and "do work" that is given to them by teachers. When they turn 5 or 6 most children will start school and then what happens to natural free play?

If a child is lucky enough to go to a fairly open, enlightened public or private school, they may have large doses of play in Kindergarten or pre-school. But it is all luck. I have seen many Kindergarten classrooms where play was frowned on and the order of the day was to sit and get through worksheets, books, and teacher talk. As children grow older the time spent playing tends to decrease, not through the choice of the child. Adults think that they have to limit play and spend more and more time on instruction. More time is spent on listening to teachers talk, doing worksheets or other written assignments, and being told to be quiet and sit down. This is unnatural learning, imposed from outside of the world of the child and actually damages and destroys creativity and eradicates natural learning.

School also often tries to take away free time on evenings and weekends. Work that is not done during the day has to be carted home and done at night. Many teachers and parents expect children to do homework every night and if they don't bring homework home they are guilty of some kind of crime. God forbid that they have any free time to play and enjoy their lives. This robs kids of more of their free time. Some children live in unsafe neighborhoods or parents have succumbed to fear of real or imagined danger and won't allow their kids to play outside. They may also be afraid of too much screen time so they won't let kids watch TV or play on the computer. Recess has been reduced over the years and in some schools free play has been replaced with structured activities. One of the most ridiculous practices that I have always opposed is that children that can't be quiet and sit still in class get their free time taken away! The only time they have to "get the wiggles out" is taken away. It is called "recess detention" and means if I don't get all of my work done or "misbehave" I have to stay in a classroom or stand on the wall outside while other children play. Then the adults wonder why some kids go nuts before the day is over. All their time to play has been taken.

Anthropologists studying hunter-gatherer cultures have noted the effects of years of free play on children. In those cultures children are allowed to do as they please just about all of the time from age 4 (when they are considered to have gained common sense) to their middle or late teens. Adults regard them as being in the process of learning to be an adult in that culture. They play with the tools of their culture: knives, fire, bows and arrows. They play games to help them learn how to hunt and interact socially with each other and the adults. As a result, they have been described as being happy, cooperative, cheerful, considerate and wonderful children and adults. No whining.

My experience is that when our modern children are given freedom to play they spend a lot of time watching videos on various topics on YouTube, playing computer games, and playing physical games either outside where they like to ride bikes, skate, run and jump, and inside where they play basketball, tag, hide and seek, soccer, wrestling and others. Less often they play cards, or board games. Sometimes they will build or play with legos or other toys. Peter Gray says that play is exploring skills needed for adulthood. So how do the activities above prepare children for adulthood? Well, obviously computers are a tool of the culture. But in all these activities if you watch closely children are talking and negotiating with each other. When we began, these exchanges were often heated, insult laden, and illogical. But the longer we have gone the more we see children reasoning with each other and compromising to get everyone farther towards whatever goal they are working towards.

In September of 2018 the American Academy of Pediatrics released a study, *The Power of Play: A Pediatric Role in Enhancing Development in Young Children.* It clearly presents the role of play in child development. The report opens with this: "Children need to develop a variety of skill sets to optimize their development and manage toxic stress. Research demonstrates that developmentally appropriate play with parents and peers is a singular opportunity to promote the social-emotional, cognitive, language, and self-regulation skills that build executive function and a prosocial brain. Furthermore, play supports the formation of the safe, stable, and nurturing relationships with all caregivers that children need to thrive. Play is not frivolous. It enhances brain structure and function and promotes executive function (i.e. the process of learning rather than the content), which allows us to pursue goals and ignore distractions."

The report continues to extol the value of free play, especially outdoor physical play. Play helps build social skills, and problem-solving skills. It encourages risk-taking, experimentation, and testing boundaries

.

At Mountain Laurel Sudbury School in Newington Connecticut they answer a question about if students ever choose to play all day, "In some cases, yes, and this is not viewed as a problem. Too often in the "adult" world, work is viewed as that which we don't want to do, but have to, while play is that which we want to do, but don't have time for. At MLSS, play is recognized not only as a valuable learning tool, but as an essential ingredient of a happy life, not only for young students, but for older ones and staff as well. As the line between work and play is blurred, students are able to graduate without the fear of (or resignation to) work or the guiltiness around play that is all too common in our society."

So let's think about free play compared with classroom instruction. Do we really want creative, critical thinkers? Do we really want problem-solvers? Or do we want docile compliant robots? Which do we really want? If we want critical thinkers who can express their ideas and back them up with reasoning, then we have to let children experience that. It can't come from adults in a transmission model. It has to come from situations that naturally arise, during the course of their natural play and interactions with others. If we want compliant children who are skilled at answering out of date questions transmitted from the teacher/standards then we are running schools correctly.

Suggestions
1. Expand play time as much as possible. Part of the day playing is better than no play at all.
2. Make sure the play is unstructured and totally free.
3. Never, ever take free play time away as a punishment for overactive children.

Chapter 5 - How much should children and their families be involved in decision-making?

Sally is a frustrated mother. Her daughter Mary is in 5th grade and is socially awkward. The other girls tend to make fun of her and make her feel isolated. Mary is very bright and reads well but gets confused in math easily. She has some anxiety and when she starts to feel especially anxious she starts pacing around in a circle. They pacing makes her feel better and she actually is better able to focus on the discussion when she is moving. The teachers, however, are always making her sit down. They can't seem to understand why she needs to pace. Sally has met with the 5th grade team and the principal but it seems out of the realm of possibility that they could let her pace when she feels anxious. "What if all the students wanted to get up and walk around?" they ask.

Boris loves motors. He likes to tinker with his 4 wheeler out in the pole barn behind the house. He has taken it apart and put it back together a hundred times. He would rather be outside, no matter what the weather is like, than be cooped up inside. Natasha loves to draw. She likes to do it on paper, or on a computer or tablet. She can spend hours creating the perfect drawing of a cat or a horse. The weird thing is she is allergic to a lot of animals and plants. She doesn't do well outdoors. Alphonse loves basketball. He can spend hours every day dribbling and shooting playing one on one or HORSE. It also helps him relax and concentrate on other things. The weird thing is when he plays basketball he feels smart and capable and powerful.

Do we want school to be a valuable experience for people who are seeking to learn? Why would we not want to take in consideration the dreams, wishes, desires, plans, and goals of our customers?

Right now schools feel bound to curriculum and standards and don't often reach out to children or families to find out what their needs and interests are. It is so ingrained in the system that you either take what school has to offer or you leave it, although depending on where you live you may not have the option to leave.

Ivan Illich in his book, *Deschooling Society*, argues that by defining education as something that is difficult and possibly impossible and can only be done at school, we create a dependency so that families see themselves as powerless in the education process. Families have been trained to accept what educators say as gospel, even when it flies in the face of reason and experience.

"All over the world the school has an anti-educational effect on society: school is recognized as the institution which specializes in education. The failures of school is taken by most people as a proof that education is a very costly, very complex, always arcane and frequently almost impossible task." Illich says.

He goes on, "School appropriates the money, men and goodwill available for education and in addition discourages other institutions from assuming educational tasks. Work, leisure, politics, city living and even family life depend on schools for the habits and knowledge they presuppose, instead of becoming themselves the means of education."

How did people become educated in the years before we had mandatory public schooling? A lot of them hung around adults and watched what they did. They spent time with their families, watched their parents and the extended family to find out what it meant to be an adult. They talked to other family members, neighbors and listened to adult conversations. Maybe they read books, magazines, or maybe they were slowly given more tasks to do on the family farm or in the family business. Think Abraham Lincoln or Benjamin Franklin.

In the past families and communities were the main forces of education in a young person's life. This may not have been ideal for everyone depending on their family situation, status in life, or area they lived, but for some it worked very well.

In the modern world we don't always have the flexibility it would take for families to educate their own children, but many do take a route called homeschooling. If homeschooling is not an option for many children, how can we take the best parts of the old way and incorporate it in our education communities? Ivan Illitch suggests that we open up businesses, government entities, and encourage many small learning "shops" where people can come and go as they please and as their needs dictate. He also suggests allowing businesses to hire children for 1 or 2 hours a day to serve in their businesses in a safe way as apprentice workers to learn more about the world of work and money.

At any rate, it would benefit schools to stop trying to pretend they know everything and enlist the help of families in the education of children. Some parents, grandparents, and other family members could even work at the school as mentors or advisers to children and bring many talents and areas of expertise to the table for children to experience.

James Comer extols family participation as a key element in school reform throughout his many books and articles on schools. In his book *Leave No Child Behind* he says, "School-based management often focuses on efficiency and instruction, rather than on the creation of a school context or culture that will support development and prevent problems. A good school context is especially useful when student, staff, parent, and community needs and activities are beyond the ordinary. A principal alone cannot effectively address a school's problems, even if they are modest or even if she has the help of assistants. It requires collaboration with parents and staff. The greater the problems, the more this is true."

Students, themselves, should be the main driving force behind decisions made about what to learn, when to learn, and how to learn it. Young children know what they are interested in and what they want to do. What do we gain by forcing them to focus on what others think they should be doing, rather than what they want to do?

If we win the battle we lessen their self-confidence and their ability to problem-solve and make decisions for themselves. If they win they become "troublemakers, rebels, discipline issues".

If you want the learner to be fully engaged in their own education, then their interests must be taken into consideration. If you want to produce a robot that does what they are told without question, then you never ask them about their interests.

Many teachers try to talk to children and find out what they like to do and what their interests are, but do these inquiries lead to any changes in the instruction offered? Hard to do that if you are blindly following a calendar aligned with standards.

In his book, *Deschooling Society*, Ivan Illich writes, "A second major illusion on which the school system rests is that most learning is the result of teaching. Teaching, it is true, may contribute to certain kinds of learning under certain circumstances. But most people acquire most of their knowledge outside school . . . ."

Suggestions
1. Stretch your comfort zone to include parents and children in decisions, whether it is in discussion, voting, or consensus.
2. If you see a problem area, ask stakeholders if they see the same problem, and what ideas they have about solutions
3. Keep checking back with stakeholders as decisions are implemented to make sure they are still on board and to proactively address concerns.

Chapter 6 - Are testing and grades necessary to determine what children have learned and guide instruction?

Bert and Ethel are Danny's grandparents. They have taken care of him since he was a baby because of his mom's struggles with drug addiction. They are puzzling over his latest report card. He is in his first quarter of 4th grade. In third grade, Danny loved his teacher and got straight A's which delighted Bert and Ethel because Danny has always struggled at school. Now in 4th grade he has one B, two C's, a D and an F in reading. But Danny loves to read. It is the one thing he really likes that relates to school. He passed the state test with a very high score in reading. What happened? Did he suddenly become worse in reading? When Bert and Ethel contact the teacher it turns out that Danny didn't complete one required book report and turned one in late. She only recorded 6 grades in reading during the first quarter so when she averaged in a zero and a 50% for being late his overall score went down to 59%.

In spite of our best interests to give children freedom to learn and play and grow, there is a nagging insecurity about whether or not learning will really happen. Will they make good choices? Will they learn all the bits of knowledge that they will need in the future? How will we know if we need to intervene in the natural process and when to intervene?

Ivan Illich in his book, *Deschooling Society*, says "But personal growth is not a measurable entity. It is growth in disciplined dissidence, which cannot be measured against any rod, or any curriculum, nor compared to someone else's achievement."

There is a pretty common misconception that you can tell how a child is doing in school by looking at test results and/or grades. But if you really dig into the numbers you will see that they can be very deceptive and misleading.

Let's take a look at grades first. Teachers give assignments at different times, give quizzes and tests, and also may assess attitude, work habits, etc. Just from this it is easy to see how grades are a subjective not objective measure. Teachers then grade work and record grades. Usually they average a whole bunch of numbers together to come up with quarterly, semester, and yearly grades. So let's say that a teacher starts a new learning unit. Maybe the class is studying how to multiply and divide fractions. What would we expect children to know at the beginning? Some may know how to do the skill, but most won't have a clue. So, what is more important to gauge a student's ability: grades early in the unit or later? I would say later but usually the teacher just lumps it all together and averages scores at the beginning with the same weight as grades at the end. Or maybe little Jill knows how to multiply and divide fractions, but chooses to not do any of the practice work and then aces the test at the end. What should her grade be to reflect her knowledge of the skill? She could very well get an F on her report card because when you average a bunch of zeros into a 100 point scale it is almost impossible for a grade to recover. Some teachers give extra credit for being on time, or being neat, or for bringing in a box of Kleenex. Suppose a child doesn't even know how to multiply whole numbers, how will they be able to learn to multiply fractions? Grades can turn school into a game with winners and losers. If you complete all the work, on time, and do a good job feeding back material that was spoon fed to you in the first place, you should get a decent grade. If for whatever reason you don't do all of this you will get a bad grade. Grades have more to do with compliance to a set of procedures than to a person's ability to reason and solve problems.

At the Jefferson County Open School in Lakewood Colorado grades have been de-emphasized and in their place this public school pre-K to 12th grade has put demonstrated competencies through personal narration and completion of 6 major projects. From their website, is an explanation of the process, "Students graduate from JCOS on the basis of demonstrated competencies rather than the more traditional "seat time" and grades which add up to what is commonly known as Carnegie units or credits.

- ☐ Open School classes are both ungraded and non-graded:
  - ☐ Ungraded: Students write narrative self-evaluations in order to

complete classes and teachers respond indicating whether a student has achieved an appropriate level of proficiency.

☐ Non-graded: Students enroll in a multi-aged grouping such as Early Learning Center (typically grades 1-3) or Pre-Walkabout (typically grades 7-9), and the vast majority of course offerings are multi-aged.

☐ Students are not expected to graduate in a specified time period but are expected to remain at JCOS until sufficient personal, social, and intellectual growth has taken place."

Standardized testing has been promoted as a way to measure learning and progress. It is a severely flawed and limited way to measure a human being. For several hours a student sits and answers questions and solves problems. They may suffer from test anxiety. They may have forgotten to eat breakfast that day. Maybe mom or dad yelled at them on their way out the door. Also some people are not good at paper and pencil tasks. Let them talk to you about a problem or work with their hands and they can be very successful. Realistically, which mode is most used in our society, business, and industry today: paper/pencil, or verbal/hands on? So which style of evaluating a person would best predict their future success; testing or having conversations?

Anya Kamenetz wrote an entire book on standardized testing called *The Test, Why our Schools are Obsessed with Standardized Testing - But you don't have to be.* She goes into great detail about the history of testing and some of the political motivation behind tests. She identifies ten problems with standardized testing: 1. We're testing the wrong things. 2. Tests waste time and money. 3. They are making students hate school and turning parents into preppers. 4. They are making teachers hate teaching. 5. They penalize diversity. 6. They cause teaching to the test. 7. The high stakes tempt cheating. 8. They are gamed by states until they become meaningless. 9. They are full of errors and 10. The next generation of tests will make things even worse.

We feel a constant need to measure and check on a person's progress. Is this really necessary? What will it take for us to relax and allow a person to come into their own set of skills naturally in their own time?

Larry Cuban writes in the book *School, The Story of Public Education,* "The scanty evidence available on whether standardized test scores are connected to job performance suggests that they are not linked."

The Myths of Standardized Tests, Why They Don't Tell You What You Think They Do authors Phillip Harris, Bruce M. Smith, and Joan Harris, Rowman quote a Leonard Baird study from 1985,"The most efficient information for predicting future accomplishments is data on previous accomplishments. The studies reviewed here show that the best predictors of future high-level, real-life accomplishment in writing, science, art, music and leadership are similar accomplishments, albeit at a lower level, in previous years ....[T]he most effective predictor of high-level accomplishments is past high-level behaviors of the same or similar types."

In our alternative program we have done away with grades totally. No complaints from parents or kids. We are constrained to take standardized testing because we are a part of a public school corporation, but if I had my preferences we would do away with that. I know much more about the children that work with me every day than any test will ever reveal. Tests are very limited because they only measure certain kinds of knowledge. They are limited to artificial problems which have to be solved in a particular way. The test makers, of course, are looking for one right answer, although they do allow for a few different methods to arrive at that answer.

Have you ever read a standardized test? Try taking a sample online sometime - they are readily available. Dull stories and inane questions abound. How do these low interest tests really measure someone's learning?

Testing is a multi-billion dollar industry and like many elements of our establishment today are really designed to enrich corporations more than help children and adults at school.

One thing I would really like us to think about is why we want to keep the test questions a deep dark secret. What purpose does this really serve? If a test is supposed to measure learning and problem-solving ability, shouldn't the question be known ahead of time? Should test-takers be able to use all their skills and talents to research the question and find the best answer? Isn't that what we would do in the workplace?

One reason the questions have to be secret is that they are the property of the testmaking corporation and if questions were open to the public, not only would the public see how ridiculous they are, the corporation would lose their monopoly and their very reason for existence.

At the very least, all state legislators and state department of education personnel should be required to take and pass a version of the state test before they can make regulations regarding student testing.

Fairtest, the website for the National Center for Fair and Open testing lists these principles which guide their work,

"Assessments should be fair and valid. They should provide equal opportunity to measure what students know and can do, without bias against individuals on the bases of race, ethnicity, gender, income level, learning style, disability, or limited English proficiency status.

Assessments should be open. The public should have greater access to tests and testing data, including evidence of validity and reliability. Where assessments have significant consequences, tests and test results should be open to parents, educators and students.

Tests should be used appropriately.
Safeguards must be established to ensure that standardized test scores are not the sole criterion by which major educational decisions are made and that curricula are not driven by standardized testing.

Evaluation of students and schools should consist of multiple types of assessment conducted over time. No one measure can or should define a person's knowledge, worth or academic achievement, nor can it provide for an adequate evaluation of an institution.

Alternative assessments should be used.
Methods of evaluation that fairly and accurately diagnose the strengths and weaknesses of students and programs need to be designed and implemented with sufficient professional development for educators to use them well."

Suggestions

1. Don't teach to the test. It has been shown that student do worse on assessments

when they are stressed out. Over emphasis on tests may actually be counterproductive.

2. If you have to give tests, limit the number and the length.

3. Parents may consider withdrawing students during testing windows or asking that their children not participate in the test. Laws vary by state, so check into possible consequences.

Chapter 7 - Does coercion and compliance lead to good citizenship and a happy life?

There is going to be a battle in the cafeteria today and everyone knows it. Tina loves to wear her hood over her hair in lunch and Ms. Massey, the assistant principal is going to tell her to take it off. Tina is just coming back to school after a 5 day suspension from the last time she told Ms. Massey very rudely and profanely that she was not going to take her hood off, that Ms. Massey was not her mother, and that Ms. Massey couldn't make her take it off no matter what she said. Tina relishes these battles, while Ms. Massey dreads them. Tina doesn't mind days off school because her mom has to go to work so Tina can lay on the couch and watch TV, surf the net, and even go outside if it is nice enough. School is boring anyhow. Ms. Massey can't seem to figure out how to avoid the battle of wills.

At school we take away many human rights from children in the name of order. Is it worth it? Some children don't mind complying with orders. We politely call it "following directions" like we were reading recipes off a box of cake mix. We want children to sit still while adults cram thoughts, lessons, and standards into their young brains. Children who come to school with curiosity and a desire to learn are made to feel like failures, because to be a success they have to comply with what others want them to do. To be successful they must kowtow to authority figures instantly with no question and no complaint.

What if, instead of instant compliance, we helped children develop their natural questioning skills? Can we help them politely, intelligently, logically question authority? Aren't we better off this way? Do we want children growing into adults who don't ask questions, who do what they are told without thought?

I have often maintained you can break children down into several groups. There are those who love being told what to do, love playing the school game and excel in traditional classes. They not only excel, they thrive. Another group is the quiet group who never complains, never act out, but may also never celebrate or find joy. The third group is the rebel group, who are unhappy and don't try to keep it a secret. The first two groups tend to make it through, but is this environment really beneficial to them? What will they do with their lives when they become adults? Will they be able to find jobs where someone will be telling them what to do all the time? In the 21st Century, won't most employers want workers who show initiative and ask questions?

James Comer, a doctor and education reformer points out in his book, *Leave No Child Behind, Preparing Today's Youth for Tomorrow's World* that our current system was based on needs of the machine age and that not all students were successful in the system and even fewer students today will thrive under the system. "Today even fewer will sit and take in what they often consider to be irrelevant information when there are so many exciting opportunities for learning outside of school. Also we send a double and confusing message. We praise children for being active learners and expressive people outside of school yet expect them to be docile learners inside."

Even if your job demands compliance, what about your duties as a citizen? Would we like to see more people take part in politics? Would we like more people exercising their right to vote? Wouldn't it be great if more quality people ran for office? Do we want citizens who blindly follow authority figures or do we want citizens who thoughtfully question everything they hear whether it is from the government or news sources?

Honestly, I think some of our leaders are perfectly satisfied to have an electorate who are docile and controllable or who don't participate.

Jerry Mintz points out in his excellent book, *School's Over* that children often act out with extreme behavior just so they don't lose their own identity. He writes, "Sometimes they pour so much of their energy into fighting authority figures that they almost can't hear what the authority figures are saying to them, they just know they don't want to accept it because it is coming from the "enemy"."

Many people in our society feel inferior. They feel like they don't have a place, that they don't have a meaningful life. We tell children that if they follow directions, stay out of trouble, get good grades, graduate, go on to college, and get a degree or degrees then they will have a good life. But what if I don't get good grades? What if I don't behave according to the adult-imposed rules? It can seem like I don't have value, that I am a failure, all because I don't fit the mold. The truth is that following the compliance school path does not guarantee anything. Even getting college degrees does not even guarantee anything other than crushing student debt.

In traditional schools peace and quiet are vastly overrated. I have come to believe that to keep a child's brain active and growing means keeping them engaged in activities that they value, even if it is conflict. This may mean some degree of noise and confusion. Have you ever noticed that adults have similar difficulties when they gather in groups? It is hard (maybe impossible) to sit in a meeting, sporting event, concert, etc and not talk to the people around you, or get up and move around.

In the new economy of the 21st Century people will need to forge a path that may include working in traditional jobs, navigating the gig economy, starting their own business, working in a co-op or other non-traditional business setup. Can schools help children grow into productive, contributing adults? Do we want compliant robots or creative citizens who participate fully in all the systems that we hope will lead to a brighter future?

Why are schools so afraid of disobedience, non compliance, disagreements? Why can't we extend the same rights to children that we take for granted as adults? Why should there be a penalty if children opt out of activities that we have so meticulously planned for them?

What if the very thing we insist that they do actually lowers performance on assessments? What if our insistence on compliance is actually a barrier to learning? Let's say I have planned fun spelling games leading up to a spelling test on Friday. 10 kids opt out all week. I give the test on Friday and then I get similar results to what I get when I insist everyone comply. Does that mean I wasted my time designing all those activities? Or could I have let kids opt out and come up with their own strategy for learning the words? Or could I have let them choose their own words? Or could I have allowed them to do what they wanted and put the activities out as a choice and then see what happened? But we are so wrapped up in getting kids to do what we think is optimal that we miss opportunities to engage with students in authentic learning and decision-making opportunities.

Recently I worked with a girl who stated she wanted to learn algebra. We did some problems together and then I gave her some practice. We corrected errors together. I didn't give her a score. The learning was more authentic because she asked for it. She was free to stop at any time. Our work together led to doing some fact practice as I detected that she was still a bit slow at some basic calculations.

Suggestions
1. Encourage children to ask questions and train adults to answer them in a respectful way or direct children to sources so they can answer their own question.
2. If a child has a complaint or challenges a procedure or rule, don't treat it as a discipline issue. Give the child a response based on logic and if possible find a compromise or consensus of all affected people, adults and children.

3. Give students a major role in decision-making process. Give the people most affected by decisions a way to influence those decisions.

Chapter 8 - Do we need school buildings and classrooms?

Kids ride bikes up and down the long driveway. Kids explore the woods and jump on rocks and climb trees. Kids sit on couches and easy chairs to discuss a book they have all decided to read. Two kids stand behind another and watch as she navigates her way through the world of a video game. Several kids measure ingredients to make a batch of cookies. They purchased all the supplies themselves and plan to sell the cookies to raise money for a museum trip. Why do these kids need classrooms?

Tom never has done well in school. He marches to the beat of his own drummer. He doesn't like sitting at a desk listening to the teacher talk. He can only take so much of that before he has to get up and leave. He is not polite about it either. He just gets up and walks out. If he is challenged by the teacher he will say, "This is boring. You're stupid. I'm leaving." He will then walk down to visit the people in the office. They are busy working however and soon become impatient with him. He sometimes kicks the furniture or uses bad language and ends up suspended. He has a very active brain however and loves to sit and play games on the computer or watch videos about animals, dinosaurs, or videos of other people playing computer games. When you can get him to have a conversation with you he has a lot of information about a wide variety of subjects.

School buildings are built to support the traditional system of kids divided up by age into groups of 20-30 who work pretty much in lockstep all day long. At some point they may go to the gym or the cafeteria or outside to the playground for a prescribed period of time. When you walk into most schools you see a space divided up into boxes.

Schools look pretty much the same although some are newer or prettier or older or uglier but form follows function and the function was determined long ago to be the production of a product in assembly line fashion.

There was a period of time in the 1970's and 1980's when some schools were opened up.

The open concept for the most part did not succeed because instruction didn't change. The teachers still wanted to be able to lecture large groups and maintain quiet. The open concept worked better when the adults were open to changing their instructional practices.

In some parts of the world classrooms have moved outdoors. Outdoor and wilderness education exist in many locations. The website outdoored.com lists 63 pages of outdoor schools who serve people from 1.5 years old to college age.

At Workspace Education in Bethel Connecticut, the space is arranged like a modern shared workspace that many businesses are moving to, where people rent space and can share ideas and help each other. At Workspace Education families can design the learning environment that works best for their child. Workspace also houses two micro schools, Acton Academy and Prism Academy each designed to meet special needs of children.

There have sprung up in different places adventure playgrounds where children have the freedom to move about and use various tools to build their own structures.

In 1967 Max Wolff proposed the idea of educational parks where a group of school buildings could share a campus and provide a bigger variety of opportunities for children.

Ivan Illitch talks about educational networks in his book, *Deschooling Society*. Written in 1970 he uncannily foreshadows the World Wide Web when he talks about giving everyone access to experts and knowledge.

Many of our communities have empty buildings that could be used to offer a variety of small schools. We spend millions of dollars on school buildings that house large numbers of kids. Why not look at some different ways including outdoor?

The Capital Region Education Council in Harford Connecticut has established 15 magnet schools that appeal to different kinds of learners. Several arts schools exist, but there are also Montessori, Reggio Emila, science, global studies and also an elementary program based on museum studies. The next step could be to expand programs into authentic locations.

In a few places nomadic schools have been established, where learners meet at a designated place in the morning and then travel to various locations, following the whims and wishes of whoever shows up that day.

What reason do we have for school building and classrooms other than tradition? Is it really the best setting to further student learning?

One force that may limit the future of school buildings is technology. It is not really necessary any more for a student to travel to a particular building to gain knowledge. They can do it from their home, church, or local Starbucks.

Technology can be a wonderful addition to school. But it is only a tool. If you don't have a philosophy that is adjustable to all learning styles and circumstances, technology will just become another brick in the wall. It will become another way to deliver instruction that is meaningless and irrelevant to the lives of the children.

So if we say, "Hey kids, let's do this cool math game," and when they are not interested, either coerce or bribe them to do it, then we are misusing technology.

However, I have seen kids jump on a game because other kids were playing it and having fun. It is great to be able to provide the most updated and recent technology possible so that kids can explore their world unfettered by glitches and slowdowns, but it is also good to allow children to experience frustration and have them use their problem-solving skills to work their way out of difficulties.

Technology can also be used to individualize and personalize learning. Usually children are very proficient with electronics and are eager to do certain things. To the dismay of certain adults, what they want to do does not often jibe with what the adults want. They, of course, love social media, video games (often violent), watching videos, listen to music.

Technology in its essence is a force for freedom. It could be the force that breaks the state monopoly on the tools of learning. Most people carry in their pocket a personal computer more powerful than a room size computer in 1960. All the knowledge of the ages, every book ever written, every song ever composed, every movie or TV show ever shown is available on that personal computing device. Are we really going to continue to pretend that books and schools are the only way to gain knowledge?

Suggestions

1. Look around your community/school system and see if there are buildings or places that are not being used that might offer some unique learning locations.
2. Take your class outdoors for half a day or maybe even all day.
3. Check out local parks/museums. Often there are great learning opportunities available.

Chapter 9 - Do we need to supervise children to keep them safe?

Bernice loves to flip on the playground, but it just about gives her kindergarten teacher a heart attack every time she does it. "Bernice! Stop that is not safe," Mr. Kelly yells, running over to the slide. Bernice is puzzled. Why is it not safe? She does it all the time at home. When she asks Mr. Kelly he says that others might try it and they wouldn't know how to do it. Bernices answers, "But I would help them learn."

In his book, *Weapons of Mass Instruction*, John Taylor Gatto relates story after story about people (some famous and some not) who did not finish school but became successful. One remarkable story is about Sir Richard Branson, who started multiple businesses including Virgin Records, Virgin Airline, and private space company Virgin Galactic. He was a dropout and started his first business at age 16. When he was four years old, his mother drove him into a

London suburb, miles from home, and asked him if he could find his way home, when he said yes, she told him to get out and do it! And he did! At age 12 he was making 100 mile bike trips.

He says on the virgin website, "You don't learn to walk by following rules. You learn by doing, and by falling over."

At Summerhill in England, Sudbury Valley School in Massachusetts and many others students are unsupervised by adults a large part of the time. Part of learning to be an adult in the culture you live in is to take risks and find out the limits of your ability and strength. We all must conquer fear in order to be effective in our modern world.

Peter Gray also addresses this issue in *Free to Learn*, pointing out that we learn to become effective adults through playing with the tools of our culture, and we need time alone or with our peers, unfettered by adults. He and his wife allowed their son to take a trip to England when he was in his teens. He earned the money himself, arranged to stay at various locations, and managed his own special medical condition.

Louis L'Amour, famed western author, in his book, *Education of a Wandering Man*, talks about how he left school at age 15 to travel the United States and the world. He worked in a variety of jobs, went to sea, and had many astonishing experiences. One time he was working as a mine attendant in Death Valley California. When the owner of the mine failed to come pick him up, he set out in a model T Ford. When the car broke down he was forced to walk out, with almost no supplies and a sketchy knowledge of the water holes in the area. He made it out, relying on his knowledge and strength as an individual.

Sometimes we treat children as if they are made of glass and worry that if we don't watch them every second that they will injure themselves. I think in some cases children may be more willing to engage in physical aggression towards each other when there are adults hovering around, because they know that the adults will intervene if things get out of hand. I started to wonder why they don't come in after a weekend off or a holiday break bruised, with black eyes, and broken limbs. Maybe it is because they are capable of keeping themselves safe. But if we always prevent them from experiencing danger and engaging in risky business, how will they find out their abilities, their limits, and their inner strength?

We don't want to leave them totally on their own. As adults we have a responsibility to keep them safe and to intervene when they make bad decisions based on their lack of experience, but that doesn't mean we have to supervise them all the time. At Sudbury Valley School they have a certification system where children can be certified to go to local stores, use tools, and other risky activities by taking a class or by taking a test.

But at traditional school it is considered a crime to leave a child alone even for a few minutes.

How much supervision a child needs varies from child to child and adult to adult, but they should be able to enjoy time by themselves.

Suggestions

1. Talk to parents and kids to see if there are any activities that they feel comfortable with children being unsupervised.
2. Leave groups unsupervised for short periods of time and gradually lengthen them.

3. Set ground rules and expectations for activities and have groups self-evaluate on how well they did.

Chapter 10 - Is the best way to learn is to sit and listen to a teacher talk?

What do you remember about school? Do you remember that lecture your teacher used to teach you about adding, subtracting, the civil war, prepositions, etc etc? Or do you remember recess, crushes, plays, music concerts, games and competitions? How much time do teachers spend talking at your school? How long do students have to sit and listen? What are they really thinking about when they sit and get? Sit in the back of a classroom sometime and watch what kids do when the teacher is talking. What can you tell by their actions, body movement, eyes? Are they toying with things in or on their desk? Are they looking at the teacher or out the window? What happens when someone walks by in the hall?

Ron Paul in his book *The School Revolution* makes this point, "But the idea that the lecture is a good way to communicate basic information, most of which is supposed to be remembered, is ludicrous. We know this because at least 90 percent of everything in a lecture is forgotten in less than three weeks." He goes on to observe, "That is why classroom instruction is a poor substitute for reading." I would take the word "reading out of the quote and substitute the word "living".

In *The New School* Glenn Harlan Reynolds talks about how online learning including Khan Academy could revolutionize learning for little cost or free. When students view a video or do online learning, they can replay the experience, back it up, and play it over and over again until they get what they want out of the experience.

When you think about learning you must think about brains. What model best represents what happens to a brain when learning is taking place?

Is the brain a cup or a bottle that you fill with knowledge? The adult pours knowledge into the child's brain until it begins to overflow. And then what? Empty some out to make more room. This idea seems very flawed and I don't think it really reflects what goes on.

Is the brain a sponge that absorbs anything liquid in the general vicinity? Again what happens when you fill the sponge and the liquid starts to leak all over? Again I would reject this model for the same reasons as the cup, although it might explain why we tend to forget things we learn.

Is the brain a plant that grows and changes over time? Sunlight and moisture and nutrients nourish the plant and it gets bigger and bigger to the limits of its species? Maybe a little better of an analogy. Brain research has shown that when you learn something new you grow a new dendrite. This is explained in an online series entitled "The Science of Learning" on the Envision Blog, "You are born with at least 100 billion brain cells, called **neurons**. As you listen to, talk about, or practice something, fibers called **dendrites** grow out of your neurons. Learning is built, as your network of dendrites grow higher and higher, with new dendrites sprouting from existing dendrites. In other words, you're building new knowledge upon the things you already know (like a tree sprouting twigs from existing branches)." This is all fine but it still doesn't explain everything. The theory expounded in the article is that you have to connect learning to stuff people have already learned so how do you learn something new? I think the brain as a plant is a better model than the cup or the sponge, but maybe not the best.

Is the brain a muscle that you can build through exercise and training so that when it meets a new situation, it can bring to bear its past work on the new problem? I favor this last idea and it seems to have been borne out by my own experience with children. In our first year of self-directed learning 19 out of 22 of our students improved in reading by an average of 18 points. The expected gain is 9. In math they gained 16 points and the expected gain is 12. This was with little or no formal instruction in those areas. We did some one on one reading and math with some kids, but not much. I wasn't surprised with the results, but some of my colleagues in other schools were. In reflecting on why this happened the only thing I can come up with is that our kids spend all day having conversations, negotiating and playing with each other and adults, watching videos, making things, playing computer games, riding bikes and skateboards or just hanging out with their friends and having fun. In all of this they are constantly working that brain muscle in a variety of ways. Just making choices and trying to figure out what they are going to say or do next is great brain exercise apparently.

What qualities will our children need to be successful in the future?

In 2008 IBM released a study that resulted from a survey of 1000 CEOs from around the world. It was entitled "The Enterprise of the Future". Here are some of the results.

"The Enterprise of the Future is capable of changing quickly and successfully. Instead of merely responding to trends, it shapes and leads them. Market and industry shifts are a chance to move ahead of the competition."

"The Enterprise of the Future surpasses the expectations of increasingly demanding customers. Deep collaborative relationships allow it to surprise customers with innovations that make both its customers and its own business more successful. "

"The Enterprise of the Future radically challenges its business model, disrupting the basis of competition. It shifts the value proposition, overturns traditional delivery approaches and, as soon as opportunities arise, reinvents itself and its entire industry"

"The Enterprise of the Future goes beyond philanthropy and compliance and reflects genuine concern for society in all actions and decisions."
Notice the key words in the IBM study, "Change, collaboration, disruption, genuine concern for society" These are characteristics that come from children learning and working together freely not by a teacher talking to them.

True learning takes a lot of thinking and work on the part of the learner and a lot of patience for people trying to facilitate learning. Unfortunately, with the way schools are set up and organized, it is hard to have patience. Sometimes people need a lot of time to get to the point where they are ready to talk, plan, and explore their ideas about what they want to learn and how they want to learn it. If you push them too soon they will rebel against interference. What right do any of us have to tell another person that they are not going fast enough towards a goal?

One of the biggest problems with top down teacher talking learning listening models of learning is the idea that human beings are always learning. It is nearly impossible to observe from the outside what and how much and how fast someone is learning. They may not even be able to articulate it themselves. There are many layers of learning. What can be observed from the outside may only be the tip of the iceberg. There are the deep levels of learning that are mostly hidden and very personal. There is the tip of the iceberg which may be measured, tested, etc most reliably through one-on-one conversation. It may be impossible for an adult in a room of 20-30 children to have time and opportunity to get at these conversations. These conversations are ones in which we express what we have learned and in the process of expressing ourselves, we create new learning in partnership with another. I have watched these conversations happen in classrooms, skate parks, gyms, swimming pools, and many other places and they often happen between people of relatively close ages.

Agile Learning Centers have a ritual where learners state an intention in the morning to a small group and then reflect at the end of the day with the same group about what actually took place. This is a great way for kids to think about their own learning and create new learning in conjunction with others, but it doesn't have much to do with sitting and listening to teachers talk.

The Macomber Learning Center in Framingham Massachusetts has this to say about their philosophy of learning, " At Macomber Center, kids are free to decide for themselves how to spend their time each day, within the bounds of community rules and norms. Our Center is a vibrant and dynamic place, and what we do here is different all the time. And, all the kids and grown-ups have their own unique perspective on what it's like to be a part of this community. We read books, play video games, build things, make music, talk to each other, and lounge in the sun. Sometimes we talk about physics and the properties of light. Sometimes we share stories about gross leftovers in the fridge. Always, we are learning: about the world, about each other, about ourselves."

One of the guiding principles stated by North Star in Sunderland, Massachusetts says, "Conventional wisdom says that children "go to school to learn," as though learning can only occur in places specially designed for that purpose. We believe that people learn all the time and in all kinds of places. It doesn't have to look like school or feel like school to be valuable, and it's not necessary to make distinctions between "schoolwork" and "your own hobbies" or "for credit" and "not for credit." As one teenager who had recently left school observed, "Everything I do counts now."

Suggestions

1. Experiment with different ways to facilitate learning with little or no teacher talk.
2. Allow students to do truly independent work, only intervening when asked to by the student.

Chapter 11 - When and how will change happen?

Is it possible that public schools will change and give families more options when it comes to education? If they want to compete I think they will have to change or they will fade away.

Schools will have to change. People who work at school have no choice. If public schools don't change drastically, they will find themselves out of business. In the book *Disrupting Class* by Clayton M. Christensen, Curtis W. Johnson, and Michael B. Horn the authors explain a force in economics called disruption. This phenomenon occurs when a monolithic organization dominates an industry and is very resistant to change. A revolutionary force can then start with a marginalized or underserved population and when a tipping point is reached can become dominant in the industry with the former leader being sent to the dust heap of history. Examples include how IBM dominated the computer business until Apple and Microsoft came along and how digital photography (and now cell phones) ruined film cameras.

What forces will emerge to disrupt compulsory public education? Public education can have some control over this if public schools become more responsive to families' needs. Charter or even formerly traditional public schools could absorb some of the disruption **if** they are true alternatives to the traditional school. If they are just more of the same thing they won't fill the needs for freedom and engagement any better than the public school does.

Home school is already a huge movement in the educational world. Of course, there are many reasons that families might choose homeschooling. It could be religious, resistance to the dominant culture for a variety of reasons, rejection of how the public school operates, the feeling that their children's needs are not being met, and others. Some may choose homeschooling to give their children the opportunity to be free.

There are private schools that offer some alternatives to traditional compulsory public education. Often they are cookie cutter copies of public schools with the control in the hands of adults, featuring sit and get lessons, emphasis on compliance to coercion.

There is a small group of schools scattered all over the world that offer more freedom. Sudbury Valley School in Framingham Massachusetts has been in existence since 1968 and offers children ages 4-20 complete freedom to pursue any interest they have. Daniel Greenburg, one of the founders of Sudbury Valley, tells the story in *A Place to Grow,* of a child who came to the school and fished every day for 2 years rain or shine, snow or sleet. He then moved on to computers and later found a job in the IT industry. Sudbury Valley has inspired schools all over the world.

Of course the grandparent of all free democratic schools is Summerhill in England. Founded by A.S. Neil in 1921 it is still a private boarding and day school that promotes freedom of children and making decisions in the democratic school meeting.

Many people have turned to Montessori schools as an alternative to traditional schooling. While there is a significant difference between Montessori and traditional school, the control still ultimately lies with the adults. Children work and play in mixed age groups. Adult staff observes them and design learning based on their demonstrated interests.

Similar to Montessori are Waldorf schools based on the work of Rudolf Steiner. Students are encouraged to follow their own interests but there is a curriculum in place that is controlled by adults.

If you look at the list of member schools on the Alternative Education Resource Organization websites, you will see that there are already a lot of amazing schools all over the world. New schools will spring up and offer amazing choices, and there are already a lot of models to copy and learn from. Below are listed some of the schools on that list.

La Cecilia School at Santa Fe, Argentina describes their program this way, "In practical terms, the school works with small groups and socio-affective grouping, flexible, with a system of open classrooms and free choice, by which children and young people can move freely through different activities. Likewise, spaces for permanent dialogue and weekly assemblies where the entire educational community participates."

Fitzroy Community School in Australia explains how their school is different, "Children spend many hours each day, over a period of 13 years, at school. These years, particularly the primary ones, are the most significant years in a child's social, ethical and emotional development. Positive development in these areas most strongly determines a child's success as a whole person. It is for this *fundamental* reason that FCS believes that the school hours each day are far too important to devote to academic proficiency alone. Academic excellence is wonderful, but this aspect of schooling is straightforward. It would be hard to equal our academic standards - but possible. However, in a hierarchy of values, FCS places *goodness* and *viability* first and foremost.

At FCS we have established a way of life which more closely reflects life in the wider world. It allows each child to be *seen* and so to come to be *known* by those of the community. It gives the young people opportunities to come *to know themselves* as they relate with a variety of others, young and old - to learn which behaviours result in positive exchanges and which lead them into unhappy situations. If you wonder why we give them free time, ask what children are like *when they are not* being told what to do. What are their strengths and weaknesses? If they can discover these, they can evolve and we can encourage their personal growth. This is the true meaning of *education* and it is a far cry from mere *schooling*."

Pine Community School is an amazing school in Queensland Australia. What follows is a part of a reflection written by a parent. "Pine's motto is "Happy Children Learn", and everything in our philosophy and approach stems from that. It starts with the well researched idea that children learn best when they are happy and relaxed and engaged – when they are actually interested in what they are doing.
So how do we make this happen? What does it mean to be happy? How do we help our children be happy, and thus learn well? For a start, Pine allows children to "have a childhood" – allowing lots of time for play, allowing them to take risks and understand consequences, not enforcing needless structure and control. We allow children to have "down time", when they're not interested in learning, and we maximize the "up time" when they're keen and excited and engaged.

Pine teachers are amazingly good at capitalizing on children's ever-changing interests. One of the many examples of this was in late 2007, when a few of the students became very interested in writing their own comic books. This was allowed and encouraged, and the interest spread, and a number of students set up their own "comic book shop" in the school's library room, spending most of each day there for a number of weeks. They defined roles for themselves (the boss, bodyguard(!), artists, writers etc), and produced comics for all the other kids to read. In this process, kids who normally hated writing were writing like crazy; kids who weren't good readers were loving reading the comics, and all the kids involved learned a lot about negotiation and teamwork."

Preshil School has existed in Melbourne Australia since 1932 and serves almost 200 students from age 3 to high school. Here is a description of their philosophy, "At Preshil, wellbeing and a confident sense of self-worth are integral to the idea of success. Academic achievement is not at the expense of health and wellbeing. The School has long been known as a centre for creativity and for a strong artistic tradition in the visual and performing arts. Our students are supported to challenge ideas, question conventional wisdom and set their own goals, qualities which are fundamental to a growth-mindset and problem solving.

Our Parents are not afraid to question mainstream schooling. They have made decisions based on strong educational ideals for their children. They are astute, well-informed people who want their children to achieve at the highest levels and they know that this should not be at the expense of their wellbeing.

Our parents do not confuse excellence in education with social status, impressive buildings or glossy marketing. They are not prepared to subject their children to a 'whatever it takes' approach to a high ATAR score and are not seeking the safety of 'the old school tie' as a pathway to a social milieu of privilege.

Our Teachers – We attract vibrant individuals who are excited to be at a school where they can really engage with their students. They want to get to know their students and help them to flourish as learners and to earn the respect of they need to be effective teachers. They set out to gain the trust and confidence students need if they are to ask for help, take up challenges and know they are acknowledged as successful learners.

The IB programmes require rigorous and ongoing professional development; our teachers engage in a global network of educators, sharing extraordinary resources and opportunities for international collaboration.

Our Students expect to be treated with respect for their individual differences. They are able to pursue their own passions in learning within a challenging and engaging curriculum. Our students formulate their own ideas, they are encouraged to question, to take risks and to make and learn from their mistakes.

They tell us that they are able to be themselves at Preshil. They have a strong sense of stewardship for the School facilities and are not prevented from 'making themselves at home."

The Peninsula School in Belize lists this goal on their website, "Our goal is to educate students to become independent thinkers, lifelong learners, to pursue academic excellence and individual achievement, in a context of respect for others and service to the community."

In Brazil there is the Laseneuax Institute where they decry the current state of education comparing it to prison. Here is how they describe their alternative program, "The Lasneaux Institute promotes a pedagogy that is organized around the concepts of autonomy and democracy. This pedagogy combines trust in human nature, a positive view of all, and free exposure of content - using a variety of forms and tools to do this [such as workshops, inverted classroom, projects, digital platform, technical exits, etc.].

Our goals are:

a) to promote autonomy and happiness of the student, by the supported self-discovery;
b) to stimulate in the student the exercise of critical thinking that will allow him to situate himself in life in a free and creative way;
c) develop the attributes of ethics, culture and social responsibility, based on democratic practices in learning.

Our thesis is that the student, in adhering to our pedagogy, can:

a) increase your curiosity;
b) increase the general interest in the propaedeutics (mathematics, physics, geography, biology, etc.);
c) increase their ability to learn;
d) have greater self-understanding;
e) develop self-security;
f) gain independence in their opinions;

g) develop their critical capacity;
h) avoid the development of various psychiatric disorders and have a full psychic health.

In this way, the student will have increased overall performance."

The ALPHA Alternative School in Toronto, Canada has been around since 1972. They describe their mission in these words, "ALPHA encourages active engagement with real and meaningful pursuits, and even the youngest children are encouraged to develop a personal sense of responsibility for their own learning. Children choose what, how, and when they learn to the greatest extent possible."

The Forest School in North Gilles Canada is a unique school that features nature education. "The Forest School is an alternative learning centre that believes learning can be a wondrous adventure, and that people learn best by doing. The programs offered are hands-on, and experiential in nature. They combine freedom with form and take place both indoors and outdoors. The Forest School facilitates learning opportunities that suit the developmental age of the students-- valuing play, exploration, creative expression and naturally including things like numeracy and literacy. The classes are mixed age and small in size. There is no testing or grading."

Kalapa Learning Community in Bogata, Columbia describes their experiential learning program this way, "The children of Kalapa learn through direct experience with activities, some self-directed and of their own choosing, and others proposed by the facilitators, depending on the age group to which they belong. The Experiential methodology starts from the premise that meaningful learning occurs when we leave our comfort zone and experience new experiences -sensory, emotional, bodily and cognitive- framed in a sense that contains them. We also believe in the value of Free Play as a space to give free rein to imagination and fantasy, learn to reconcile with children of different ages, constantly communicate their feelings and needs."

The Democratic School in Berlin Germany describes self-determined learning in these words, "At the Democratic School X, all students decide for themselves, what, when and how they learn. People are curious by nature. They want to understand the world that surrounds them and find their way around them. Therefore, it is neither necessary nor useful to force children to learn or persuade. Much of the learning takes place outside and independently of classroom situations, playing, talking about all sorts of topics, through books, magazines, and electronic media, or by students trying things out, watching others, letting oneself explain something, or something make them together. Instruction courses are just one learning option, among many others."

The Elementary School of Fourfouras in Greece has what they call the school junkyard. Here is how it is described on their website, "The School junkyard or as its known among our students "The Pirate Island" , is a place of freedom. A place where every child could be anyone. Junkyard is a place of fun and games, where characters from stories come alive. Here the kids have access in everyday materials, such us plastic tubes, woods, paper boxes, stones and things like that. With all these materials they create role based games and they have a lot of fun! "

The Indian school Sholai Cloatt is on a coffee plantation and combines some traditional instruction with organic farming, green technology, and other real life occupations.

Aventurine Adventure School in the Netherlands describes their learning environment this way, "Children at Aventurine learn from life. As much as possible, practical learning is assumed. Do things yourself, and watch with working adults. If children have played and experimented sufficiently, a lot of knowledge is available. Transferring to a more abstract level is then still a small step, and made quickly."

Riverstone Village in South Africa expounds on the value of self-directed education. Here is a quote from their website, "Inside our learning community, everyone is equal, everyone is living their lives to the full, and nobody knows what anyone else 'needs' to learn. Each person, regardless of age or 'ability', is sovereign over their own body, life, and time. It is a place of caring and respect, and mutual support, where we can learn to be 100% ourselves in ways that celebrate other people's freedom, too. Where we learn how to resolve conflict so that everybody wins. Where we learn how to communicate, so that we can be fully ourselves rather than trying to 'fit in.'"

A Place to Grow in Stroud England lists these values, "the environment allows children and adults to feel physically and psychologically safe, and know that they matter. Each child is nurtured; we aim to support the social, emotional, intellectual, and creative needs of each child. We see each child as an individual who has something to offer to the community

- we see behaviour as information about how a child is feeling. There is always a good reason for any behaviour, even if we never find out what the reason is. Our aim is for each child to be felt and known at a deep level

- there is no fixed curriculum, but there is time to play, to decide on things, to change one's mind, to go with the flow—or against it. This gives children the autonomy to develop as creative and independent thinkers. We celebrate mistakes for the true lessons they are

- we embrace a non-competitive and collaborative approach. This allows children to develop their inner strengths, lifelong passions and emotional intelligence

- we welcome the whole person and allow children time and space to work out who they really are and where they fit in. There is time for relationships to develop and individuals to grow as part of our community. Children are free to interact and develop at their own pace. Daydreaming has a meaningful place and so does playing or observing. There is time for the cultivation of awe and wonder

- we adopt a neuro-diverse approach, accepting that very few of us are neuro-typical. Children are not labelled. Each child is supported by peers and adults to understand their emotions, explore different choices, and realise the consequences

- adults adopt a reflective approach to their practice. Through regular supervision and working as a team they keep children in mind, whilst keeping themselves grounded through theory and knowledge - and gaining strength through practice, practice, practice

- adults aim to be self aware and authentic. They bring their whole selves into the space thereby modeling to the children that they too are welcome to bring their whole selves

- children work together, using democratic processes, to manage their environment and develop their community. Although some of the day has a set structure, this creates the freedom and safety for children to run the rest of the day as they wish

The Marietta Johnson School of Organic Education in Fairhope, Alabama has been around since 1907 and features natural learning with no tests and no grades from k-8th grade.

The website for the Stellar Secondary School in Anchorage, Alaska says this about its philosophy, "Stellar is a school devoted to an educational setting which fosters the creation of independent, courageous people capable of dealing with the shifting complexities of the modern world. It runs on the energy and excitement of people who have committed themselves to self-directed learning. With the support of parents and staff, it attempts to help provide students with a humane education based upon freedom and responsibility."

The Kino School in Tucson, Arizona says this on their website, "Kino's mission is to provide a school where students are given both the responsibility and the freedom that lie at the heart of being a citizen in a democratic society: a school where learning, creativity, respect for others, and community thrive and where students of all abilities succeed."

Headwaters School in Arkansas has this description on its website: "Headwaters functions as a multi-aged, mixed interest group of students cooperating with each other, with teachers, and with parents on interdisciplinary projects. Interests and abilities determine a student's level of involvement. Students participate in a variety of activities ranging from group science projects to solo creative writing tasks to yoga. They are encouraged to participate in any activity that they are capable of, and many times older students will assist younger students with projects that the young ones cannot do themselves. (With the varying ages, however, it is often the younger students will have to have a recess break before the project is completely finished!) While they may not be as "perfect" as some of the older students may like, the products of these group projects are reflections of the diversity of ages, tastes, and experiences of all the Headwaters kids. As such, they are priceless."

Celebration Education at Yucaipa California says this on their website, "Every child has their own genius. We inspire that genius by allowing each child to take the lead in their learning experiences, drawing on their innate learning tools of curiosity, exploration, and creativity. To enhance those experiences, we provide rich learning opportunities in the form of an inspiring environment, access to interesting materials, varied classes, and plentiful field trips - all tied together with exciting themes."

Diablo Valley School in Concord, California, explains part of their philosophy this way, "Our philosophy is based on the fact that children naturally want to learn the skills needed to grow into capable adults. And just like grownups, they want to be free to choose how they will become successful. At Diablo Valley School, we take this natural desire for self-direction seriously, allowing it to propel children into independent adulthood. Given the freedom to pursue their interests for as long as the interest lasts, and the structure to ensure their activities are neither infringed upon nor infringe on the rights of others, children learn what they need."

Free to Learn is an Agile Learning Community for homeschoolers in Rocklin, California. Here is how they describe themselves, "Free to learn is an independent learning community for homeschoolers and unschoolers ages 4 to 18. Our kids love learning, because they have the freedom and responsibility to design and direct their own education, govern their learning community, receive academic support and caring guidance from skilled mentors. All of this sets them up to thrive."

Grass Roots Free School in Tallahassee, Florida lists 5 points in their philosophy. "There are five basic assumptions which underlie the Grassroots School approach to education:

> 1. Feelings and Emotions (i.e. the "affective domain") are as important

in a person's development as the cognitive and physical domains.

2. The mind is naturally inquisitive, and such inquisitiveness must be allowed and encouraged to the fullest extent possible.
3. All knowledge is interrelated.
4. Each person is unique and it is fundamental in an educational setting to fully respect and honor this uniqueness.
5. We are all responsible for and dependent upon each other.

So you can see from this partial list, that there are many great schools and programs that have been around for a while or are just beginning. The changes and thought that has gone into these programs is amazing. I predict that there will be more and more as more people become aware of the great possibilities of self-directed education.

Chapter 12 - The dazzling or dismal future.

Will the schools of the future be "Another Brick in the Wall" or "Shine On You Crazy Diamond"?

If we insist on continuing this failed experiment compulsory one-size-fits-all schooling system I see a dismal future for our planet. I think the issues that divide the human race will continue to get worse. I think our selfishness and abuse of our environment will accelerate. Political apathy and rampant consumerism will become the twin gods of destruction.

In the film, "Class Dismissed", the world of homeschooling is explored. The film follows a family as they navigate their dissatisfaction with public schools into different forms of homeschooling, charter schools, and back again. They land in a really good spot for their family. For many families, homeschooling is the perfect solution to the educational needs of their children. Some homeschoolers try to recreate compulsory school in their homes. That, of course, will not address the issues raised in this book. But some families will come to realize that forced schooling is not the answer whether it is at school or at home.

But it is not inevitable. We can avoid a dismal future if we will reject or severely curtail compulsory traditional schooling. Let's give families as many choices as we can devise including traditional, progressive, and self-directed options, both at schools or centers and homes.

Let's open up our cities, towns, and countryside and realize we don't have to have a special building for learning. Learning can occur at the mall, at the barbershop, at the stone quarry, at the local nature or environmental center.

We have to figure out how to make quality education available to all, regardless of zip code, parent income, citizenship, skin color, or nationality. Many conservatives have advanced the idea of vouchers or education savings accounts giving families more choices for their child's education. I think this idea has some merit, as long as it has built-in provisions for poor and working families to be able to take advantage of it. Public schools are not for every child and having more options is not a bad thing. The problem with vouchers now is that they are a smoke screen to promote racism, classism, and drain money from public schools. The biggest barrier to participation for a lot of families is transportation to the desired school.

I would love to see a plethora of small schools with 100 students or less popping up at libraries, museums, storefronts, outdoor spaces, churches, homes, or anywhere. Depending on the structure of the school, small adult staffs could serve the needs of the kids. Depending on the location of the school they could provide quality results for a low cost compared to the cost of public schools with their massive buildings and large staffs. If these small schools or learning centers did not please their customers they would go out of business because families would go elsewhere. They would vote with their feet.

Ann Arbor Open School is an example of a public K-8 school that has freedom, multi-age classrooms, is run democratically and boasts way above average test scores on the Michigan state test. This shows that if we let ourselves think outside of the box, we can achieve great things.

References

Schools referenced:

Sudbury Valley School, Framingham, Massachusetts, https://sudburyvalley.org/
ILEAD, Lancaster, California, https://ileadschools.org/
Ann Arbor Open School, Ann Arbor, Michigan, https://www.a2schools.org/aaopen
Beacon Self-Directed Learning Center, New Haven, Connecticut, http://www.beaconlearning.org/
De Riumite Soest, Soest, Netherlands, https://deruimtesoest.nl/
Mountain Play Place, Irvine California, https://www.playmountain.org/
Open School, Orange, California, http://openschooloc.com/wp/
Mountain Laurel Sudbury School, Newington, Connecticut, http://mountainlaurelsudbury.com/
Jefferson County Open School, Lakewood Colorado, https://jcos.jeffcopublicschools.org/home
Capital Regions Education Council, Hartford Connecticut, http://www.crecschools.org/our-schools
Workspace Education, Bethel, Connecticut, https://workspaceeducation.org/
Summerhill School, Suffolk England, http://www.summerhillschool.co.uk/

Macomber Learning Center, Framingham, Massachusetts, http://macombercenter.org/
North Star, Sunderland, Massachusetts, http://www.northstarteens.org/#learningisnatural
Fitzroy Community School, North Fitzroy, Victoria, Australia, http://www.fcs.vic.edu.au/
La Cecilia School, Santa Fe, Argentina http://lacecilia.org.ar/wordpress/
Pine Community School, Arana Hills, Australia http://www.pinecommunityschool.org/
Preshil Independent Progrssive School, Melbourne, Australia http://www.preshil.vic.edu.au/
Lasneaux Institute, Brasilia, Brazil, https://www.institutolasneaux.com.br/iasnaia-poliana
Peninsula International Academy, Belize, https://peninsulaacademy.shutterfly.com/
Alpha Alternative School, Toronto Canada, http://schools.tdsb.on.ca/alpha/
The Forest School,South Gilles, Canada http://www.theforestschool.ca/
Demokratische Schule X, Berlin Germany, https://www.demokratische-schule-x.de/
Elementary School of Fourfouras, Crete, Greece, https://schoolf.weebly.com/
Kalapa Learning Community, Bogata Columbia, https://www.kalapa.com.co/
A Place to Grow, Stroud England, https://www.placetogrow.org/
Aventurnine School for Adventure, Netherlands,

http://www.aventurijn.org/
Riverstone Village, Johannesburg South Africa, http://www.riverstonevillage.co.za/
Sholai Cloaat, Kodaikanal, Tamil Nadu, India, http://www.sholaicloaat.org/
Headwaters School, Pettigrew Arkansas, http://headwaters-school.org/index.html
Kino School, Tuscon Arizona, http://www.kinoschool.org/
Marietta Johnson School of Organic Education, Fairhope, Alabama, https://fairhopeorganicschool.com/
Stellar Secondary School, Anchorage Alaska, https://www.asdk12.org/steller
Celebration Education, Yucaipa, California, https://www.celebrationeducation.com/
Diablo Valley School, Concord, California, http://www.diablovalleyschool.org/
Free to Learn Agile Learning Community, Rocklin California, http://freetolearncommunity.com/
Grass Roots Free School, Tallahassee, Florida, http://www.grassrootsschool.org/

Books, articles and websites:

Source	author
Weapons of Mass Instruction,	John Taylor Gatto
What are Schools for?	Ron Miller

36 Children	Herbert Kohl
Free to Learn	Peter Gray
Disrupting Class	Clayton M. Christensen, Curtis W. Johnson, Michael B. Horn
The Anthropology of Learning in Childhood	David Lancy
The Underachieving School	John Holt
American Psychological Association website	
Sherlock Holmes is Wrong	Scott David Grey
The Power of Play: A Pediatric Role in Enhancing Development in Young Children	American Academy of Pediatrics
Deschooling Society	Ivan Illitch
Leave No Child Behind	James Comer
The Test, Why our Schools are Obsessed with Standardized Testing - But you don't have to be,	Anna Kamenetz
School, The Story of Public Education	Larry Cuban
The Myths of Standardized Tests, Why They Don't Tell You What You Think They Do, by	Phillip Harris, Bruce M. Smith, and Joan Harris
Fairtest website	The National Center for Fair and Open Testing

Leave No Child Behind, Preparing Today's Youth for Tomorrow's World,	James Comer
School's Over	**Jerry Mintz**
outdoored.com	**The Premiere Community for Outdoor Education Professionals**
The Educational Park, A Guide to its Implementation	**Max Wolff**
virgin website	**Richard Branson**
Education of a Wandering Man	**Louis L'Amour**
The School Revolution	**Ron Paul**
The New School	**Glenn Harlan Reynolds**
The Science of Learning	**Envision blog**
"The Enterprise of the Future	**ibm**
A Place to Grow	**Daniel Greenburg**
Class Dismissed	classdismissedmovie.com/

Other:

Alternative Education Resource Organization, http://www.educationrevolution.org/store/

Alliance for Self-Directed Education, https://www.self-directed.org/

Multi age classrooms
https://files.eric.ed.gov/fulltext/ED504569.pdf

Against School by John Taylor Gatto
https://www.wesjones.com/gatto1.htm

8 year study studied effect of different high school curriculum on success in college: "Moreover, the Eight-Year Study proved that many different forms of secondary curricular design can ensure college success and that the high school need not be chained to a college preparatory curriculum. In fact, students from the most experimental, nonstandard schools earned markedly higher academic achievement rates than their traditional school counterparts and other progressive-prepared students.
http://www.archive.org/stream/storyoftheeighty009637mbp/storyoftheeighty009637mbp_djvu.txt
https://www.youtube.com/watch?time_continue=379&v=0lrHG8y_9C4

Article about brain maturation rates
http://www.apa.org/education/k12/brain-function.aspx

John Taylor Gatto speech accepting teacher of the year award in 1998
http://www.naturalchild.org/guest/john_gatto.html

Waldorf Schools
https://waldorfeducation.org/waldorf_education

Self directed learning website
http://www.selfdirectedlearning.com/

Adventure playgrounds
https://www.npr.org/sections/ed/2014/08/04/334896321/where-the-wild-things-play

Open classrooms
https://calendar.google.com/calendar/r/week/2018/3/3

Life learner experience with college
http://www.lifelearningmagazine.com/1506/life-learners-path-to-college.htm